The Taiwanese Americans

The Taiwanese Americans

Franklin Ng

THE NEW AMERICANS
Ronald H. Bayor, Series Editor

GREENWOOD PRESS
Westport, Connecticut • London

Library of Congress Cataloging-in-Publication Data

Ng, Franklin, 1947–
    The Taiwanese Americans / Franklin Ng.
       p. cm.—(The New Americans, ISSN 1092–6364)
    ISBN 0–313–29762–2 (alk. paper)
    1. Taiwanese Americans. I. Title. II. Series.
  E184.T35N45   1998
  305.895'1073—dc21   97–37530

British Library Cataloguing in Publication Data is available.

Library of Congress Catalog Card Number: 97–37530
ISBN: 0–313–29762–2
ISSN: 1092–6364

First published in 1998

Greenwood Press, 88 Post Road West, Westport, CT 06881
An imprint of Greenwood Publishing Group, Inc.

Printed in the United States of America

The paper used in this book complies with the
Permanent Paper Standard issued by the National
Information Standards Organization (Z39.48–1984).

10 9 8 7 6 5 4 3 2 1

Copyright Acknowledgment

Polly Lo has given permission to use the photographs in this book.

To My Parents
Hoon Tim and Dai Moi Chun Ng

Contents

Series Foreword

Oscar Handlin, a prominent historian, once wrote, "I thought to write a history of the immigrants in America. Then I discovered that the immigrants were American history." The United States has always been a nation of nations where people from every region of the world have come to begin a new life. Other countries such as Canada, Argentina, and Australia also have had substantial immigration, but the United States is still unique in the diversity of nationalities and the great numbers of migrating people who have come to its shores.

Who are these immigrants? Why did they decide to come? How well have they adjusted to this new land? What has been the reaction to them? These are some of the questions the books in this "New Americans" series seek to answer. There have been many studies about earlier waves of immigrants— e.g., the English, Irish, Germans, Jews, Italians, and Poles—but relatively little has been written about the newer groups—those arriving in the last thirty years, since the passage of a new immigration law in 1965. This series is designed to correct that situation and to introduce these groups to the rest of America.

Each book in the series discusses one of these groups, and each is written by an expert on those immigrants. The volumes cover the new migration from primarily Asia, Latin America, and the Caribbean, including: the Koreans, Cambodians, Filipinos, Vietnamese, South Asians such as Indians and Pakistanis, Chinese from both China and Taiwan, Haitians, Jamaicans, Cubans, Dominicans, Mexicans, Puerto Ricans (even though they are already U.S. citizens), and Jews from the former Soviet Union. Although some of these people, such as Jews, have been in America since colonial times, this series concentrates on their recent migrations and thereby offers its unique contribution.

These volumes are designed for high school and general readers who want to learn more about their new neighbors. Each author has provided information about the land of origin, its history and culture, the reasons for migrating, and the ethnic culture as it began to adjust to American life. Readers will find fascinating details on religion, politics, foods, festivals, gender roles, employment trends, and general community life. They will learn how Vietnamese immigrants differ from Cuban immigrants and, yet, how they are also alike in many ways. Each book is arranged to offer an in-depth look at the particular immigrant group but also to enable readers to compare one group with the other. The volumes also contain brief biographical profiles of notable individuals, tables noting each group's immigration, and a short bibliography of readily available books and articles for further reading. Most contain a glossary of foreign words and phrases.

Students and others who read these volumes will secure a better understanding of the age-old questions of "Who is an American?" and "How does the assimilation process work?" Similar to their nineteenth- and early twentieth-century forebears, many Americans today doubt the value of immigration and fear the influx of individuals who look and sound different from those who had come earlier. If comparable books had been written one hundred years ago they would have done much to help dispel readers' unwarranted fears of the newcomers. Nobody today would question, for example, the role of those of Irish or Italian ancestry as Americans; yet, this was a serious issue in our history and a source of great conflict. It is time to look at our recent arrivals, to understand their history and culture, their skills, their place in the United States, and their hopes and dreams as Americans.

The United States is a vastly different country than it was at the beginning of the twentieth century. The economy has shifted away from industrial jobs; the civil rights movement has changed minority-majority relations and, along with the women's movement, brought more people into the economic mainstream. Yet one aspect of American life remains strikingly similar—we are still the world's main immigrant receiving nation and as in every period of American history, we are still a nation of immigrants. It is essential that we attempt to learn about and understand this long-term process of migration and assimilation.

Ronald H. Bayor
Georgia Institute of Technology

Acknowledgments

Writing a book can be a long and difficult process. I am fortunate to have had many friends, colleagues, and acquaintances who rendered help in many ways that they themselves may not have foreseen. For various insights and assistance, it is a pleasure to acknowledge my debts to Him Mark Lai, Nancy Wong, Aaron Dengler, Shien-min Jen, Susie Cheng, Robert Cheng, Wellington Chan, Alvin Y. So, Tien-yi Tao, Harry J. Lamley, Fred C. Blake, Kuo-cheng Tseng, Norman Woo, Angela Yang, Patricia Tsai, Chi Kin Leung, and Cindy Chang. Polly Lo helped to take photographs for me in Southern California, while Jennifer K. Wood, Ronald H. Bayor, Lynn Zelem, and Barbara Rader offered timely advice. Finally, I wish to give thanks to my family who patiently allowed me to take time for this book.

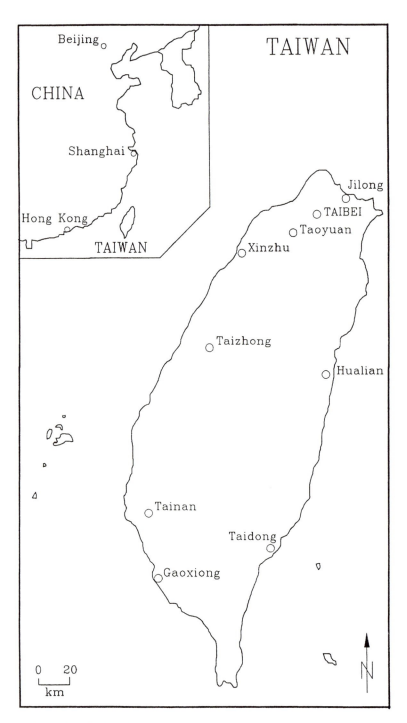

CHINA

Beijing

Shanghai

Hong Kong

TAIWAN

TAIWAN

Jilong

TAIBEI

Taoyuan

Xinzhu

Taizhong

Hualian

Tainan

Taidong

Gaoxiong

0   20
km

N

Adapted by Chi Kin Leung.

1

Introduction

WHO ARE THE TAIWANESE AMERICANS?

Since immigration law changes in 1965, the Chinese population in the United States has increased dramatically. According to the 1990 U.S. Census, there were 1,645,472 Chinese Americans. While this group includes the American-born Chinese, it also encompasses those who have migrated from Hong Kong, China, Southeast Asia, Taiwan, and other parts of the world. Taiwanese Americans, the immigrants from Taiwan and their descendants, are a prominent group in this growing Chinese population. Stories about their economic and educational successes are repeatedly touted in newspapers and magazines.

One often hears about race, ethnicity, gender, religion, and class as the significant variables in classifying people. In China, those who are ethnic Chinese are called the *Han* in contrast to the minorities that are not Chinese. But for the Chinese, native or local place identification is also important. In a country as vast as the map of Europe, there is great regional diversity. Knowledge of one's ancestral place or place of residence, which might change with time or generation, is a marker of identity. This affiliation with a geographical place of origin or residence is as vital to personal identity as one's surname. Just as the Cantonese identify with Guangdong province in Southeastern China, so the Taiwanese identify with their island home of Taiwan. Along with regional identity, there are other subcategories of geographical affiliation, such as a district, a city, or a village. With place identification also comes links with regional customs, practices, cuisines, stereotypes, and local dialects.

But the phrase "Taiwanese Americans" is far from a simple matter. There are several different meanings. First of all, in the United States, in everyday parlance or usage for many people, a Taiwanese American is anyone who immigrates from Taiwan and has become a citizen of the United States. So, it is a practical term, a term of convenience, to label those who come from that island as Taiwanese Americans. It refers to their children as well. And those who live on Taiwan are therefore often called the Taiwanese.

The term Taiwanese in this instance actually includes three different groups of Chinese: the Fujianese, the Hakka, and the mainlanders. The Fujianese are people from Fujian province who migrated to Taiwan from the sixteenth century onward and are now the majority on the island. The Hakka are a group who moved from Guangdong province to Taiwan. Finally, the mainlanders are refugees from the Chinese civil war on mainland China after World War II. Retreating before the Chinese Communists who would establish a new People's Republic of China in 1949, they withdrew to Taiwan and maintained a Republic of China in exile on Taiwan. Not usually included as Taiwanese are the aborigines, who are not considered Chinese.

On the other hand, there is also a second meaning. On Taiwan, Taiwanese is defined in a different way. Place of origin for its Han or Chinese residents is divided into two categories: Taiwan and the mainland. Those who lived on Taiwan before the end of World War II see themselves as the Taiwanese. This includes the two groups, the Fujianese and the Hakka, although the Hakka maintain an identity apart from the Fujianese majority. These Taiwanese see the immigrants coming later from the mainland after 1945 or 1949 as mainlanders. They label themselves as the *benshengren* or "local people" (literally, "people from this province"), while the mainlanders are designated the *waishengren* or "outside people" (literally, "people from outside provinces"). The aborigines are referred to as the *yuanzhu min* or "original inhabitants."

For the mainlanders, the situation is somewhat different. For many years, by their governance of Taiwan through the *Guomindang* or Nationalist Party, they have described all the Chinese population on the island as Chinese rather than Taiwanese. Use of the term Chinese accentuates their claim that there is "only one China" and not "two Chinas." It gives consistency to the Nationalist government's claim that it is the legitimate government of all the Chinese on both mainland China and Taiwan. Visitors who tour Taiwan and refer to its people as Taiwanese are sometimes reminded by officials that the proper term is "Chinese."

The distinctions between the earlier Chinese residents on Taiwan and mainlanders may undergo change in the future. After all, the mainlanders now have second- and third-generation offspring who have been born in Taiwan. Moreover, there has been marriage between the mainlanders and Taiwanese. At what point do the mainlanders become accepted as Taiwanese, merged with those who had settled in Taiwan before 1945?

The contrasting views as to what constitutes "Taiwanese" reveal an evolving identity that is changing along with historical and political circumstances. Much of this debate over Taiwanese identity, sometimes competing with a Chinese identity, relates to the politics between China and Taiwan. Anxieties about unification with China and domination of Taiwan by the larger mainland population fuel this wrestling over terms and identities. At the same time, there is lingering resentment regarding the legacy of mainlander rule over the Taiwan residents after World War II. These factors have contributed to the emergence of a stronger identity with Taiwan as opposed to China.

In this book, Taiwanese American is the term applied to immigrants from Taiwan and their descendants who are U.S. citizens. While they may belong to different groups in Taiwan, they have shared many experiences in their last country of residence. They are also familiar with the push and pull factors that attracted them to the United States. These shared experiences thus provide a common frame of reference for their later adaptation and life in America (Tseng 1995:37).

INTRODUCTION TO TAIWAN

Land

Taiwan, a large island off the southeast coast of China, is the home of the Republic of China. Many people, however, simply refer to the Republic of China as "Taiwan." Taiwan is often translated to be "Terraced Bay" or "Big Bay" in Chinese, but to the Portugese sailors who saw its verdant and pristine landscape in the sixteenth century, it was "Ilha Formosa" which can be translated as "Beautiful Island." Approximately 245 miles in length from north to south and ninety miles in width from west to east, Taiwan is closest to the mainland Chinese province of Fujian, which lies less than a hundred miles to the west (Hsieh 1964).

Several bodies of water touch Taiwan's shores. To its north is the East China Sea, separating it from the Ryukyu Islands, Okinawa, and Japan. To the south is the Baishi Channel, which lies between it and the Philippines. To the west is the Taiwan Strait or Channel that is across from mainland

China. And to the east is the vast Pacific Ocean with the Japan Current (Kuroshio), whose warm waters help moderate temperatures during winter. The water that surrounds Taiwan is important to its economy, providing it with a way to export goods and import raw materials and other products.

Taiwan is largely mountainous, especially the eastern two-thirds, which means that only about 25 percent of the land is suitable for agriculture. The western third of the island is a low, flat plain, where the majority of the people live and farm. Located in both the tropical and subtropical zones, Taiwan rests in the monsoon zone. As a result, it is visited by monsoons during the summer months from May until September. Allowing for variations in elevation, the weather is often warm and humid. The abundant rainfall supplies ample water for agricultural crops and aquaculture. It also helps to provide inexpensive hydroelectric power for the island's residential and industrial needs. On the whole, the vegetation and animals on the island are similar to those of Southern China and the Philippines.

Taiwan today also encompasses a number of island groups. Including Taiwan proper, there are twenty-two islands in the Taiwan group. In the Pescadores or Penghu group, there are sixty-four. Quemoy (Jinmen) and Matsu (Mazu) are the other two island groups. The total land mass amounts to 13,900 square miles, making it larger in size than Belgium but slightly smaller than North Korea. The main island of Taiwan has many scenic spots; among the most famous are the spectacular Taroko Gorge and the beautiful Sun Moon Lake.

People

The population of Taiwan totals 21 million people. Slightly less than 85 percent were born in Taiwan as the descendants of earlier Chinese immigrants from the mainland China provinces of Guangdong and Fujian. They are thus often called the Taiwanese. Another 14 percent are people who were born on mainland China and moved there in the period after World War II. Also ethnically Chinese, they hail from many different provinces of China. But because they came much later, withdrawing to Taiwan to escape the victorious Communist Chinese armies, they are called the mainlanders. Finally, there are the aborigines, the original inhabitants of the island before the Chinese came, who constitute about 1 percent of the population.

The term "Taiwanese" today is taken to mean the Fujianese and the Hakka (Kejia) or "guest people." The Fujianese are those who originally came from Fujian, the southeastern Chinese province closest to Taiwan. The Hakka are a people with their own dialect, who migrated into Guangdong from Henan in central China. Many later moved to Taiwan in the sixteenth and seventeenth centuries onward, and their descendants still maintain a separate identity from the other Taiwanese from Guangdong and Fujian. The aborigines, on the other hand, are related to the Malay people in Indonesia, Malaysia, and the Philippines. They speak languages classified as Austronesian or Malayo-Polynesian. There are several tribes, but the larger ones who comprise the majority are the Ami, Atayal, and Paiwan. Among the others are the Saisiat, Yami, Ruyuma, Rukai, Bunun, and Tsou. Whereas some of the tribes once lived on the western plains portion of Taiwan, many today reside in the mountainous and hilly eastern two-thirds part of the island. The number of aborigines is estimated to be over 330,000.

Taiwan has a number of large cities, all of which are concentrated on its western plains. Taibei (Taipei), the most populous city with 2.7 million residents, is the capital for the Republic of China. Located in the northern part of Taiwan, it has a population slightly less than that of Chicago, Illinois. Gaoxiong (Kaohsiung) in southwestern Taiwan is the second most populous city with more than 1.5 million inhabitants. The site of the largest seaport in Taiwan, it holds the fourth largest container port in the world. The third largest city is Taizhong (Taichung), situated in central Taiwan with 805,000 residents. Tainan, in southern Taiwan, is the next largest city with a population of over 700,000.

Language

Aside from the aborigines, the population on Taiwan is Chinese. They speak Mandarin Chinese, which is based on the Beijing dialect and is taught in the schools and universities on Taiwan as *guoyu* or the "national dialect." Mandarin is also the official dialect used on mainland China, where it is known as *putonghua* or "common language." In Singapore, where the dialect is widely used, it is referred to it as *huayu* or the "language of the Chinese." And in Hong Kong, the Mandarin dialect is named *guoyu* or "national language," as in Taiwan.

While all the Chinese on Taiwan speak Mandarin, most speak other dialects at home and outside of school. The second most widely used dialect is Hokkien (Fujian), often dubbed "native Taiwanese." Spoken by the Fujian Taiwanese and the Hakka, it is based on the Minnan dialect from southern Fujian. In addition to speaking Hokkien, many Hakka speak their own Hakka dialect. Finally, the mainlanders can converse in the regional dialects from the different provinces of China. This ability to speak two or more dialects is a characteristic that can be found among the people in mainland China as well.

Mandarin Chinese generally uses four tones. These are varying pitches attached to a sound that can give it a different meaning. Thus, the sound "ma" with four different tones can mean "mother," "hemp," "horse," and "to curse." By using different tones attached to sounds, the speaker is able to distinguish between homonyms such as "wood" and "would," or "our" and "hour," in English.

In China, the written characters have long been a glue that helped to bind the Chinese people together. China was a vast country with a wide range of spoken dialects, and many of them were not comprehensible to those who came from a different region. So often the only way that people could communicate with one another was to resort to the writing of Chinese characters. Despite the diversity of spoken dialects, the written Chinese characters usually conveyed the same meaning to everyone. In Taiwan, most people are literate in the reading and writing of Chinese characters, thanks to the emphasis on education and literacy. But because it is a separate linguistic community, there are phrases and idiomatic expressions found on Taiwan that are different from those of mainland China. Moreover, Taiwan uses traditional Chinese characters, while the mainland has adopted simplified Chinese characters to help promote literacy among its more than one billion people.

Religion

The Chinese have traditionally talked about Confucianism, Daoism (Taoism), and Buddhism as the *sanjiao*, translated as the "three religions" or "three teachings." Respect for Confucianism, however, was more for its philosophy and outlook on life than for its being seen as a religion. Confucianism valued family, filial piety, reverence for ancestors, morality, and education. Its ideas have helped shape Chinese society through the ages, but it also has immense appeal in other Asian countries such as Japan, Korea, Vietnam, and Singapore. Throughout Taiwan, there are many Confucian temples erected to commemorate Confucius and his teachings.

On the other hand, Daoism and Buddhism are major religions on Taiwan. Throughout Taiwan, there are many Daoist and Buddhist temples. Daoism has traditionally been attributed to two teachers, Laozi and Zhuangzi. Daoism as a worldview emphasizes living in harmony with nature and the cosmos. It embraces ideas of simplicity, naturalness, spontaneity, and primitivity. In other words, it teaches that people should learn to join with the natural flow of the universe. Buddhism, in contrast, teaches how people can escape pain and suffering by curbing their desires and wants. By accumulating merit and by turning to bodhisattvas or enlightened buddhas-to-be, they can achieve nirvana and obtain release from pain and suffering.

In religious practice, the Chinese have tended to fuse Confucianism, Daoism, and Buddhism. This religious synthesis or syncretism is commonly referred to as Chinese popular religion. On Taiwan, it is an amalgam of the worship of ancestors, local and city gods, other deities, bodhisattvas, and buddhas blended together. Visits to Daoist and Buddhist temples reveal this hybrid character. Among the most popular of the deities on Taiwan is Mazu (Matsu), also known as Tianhou or "Empress of Heaven." A benefactor to sailors and fishermen, she later became deified as a popular goddess and is much revered in Fujian province and Taiwan. Next to representations of Mazu are two assistant deities, "Eyes That Can See a Thousand Miles" and "Ears That Can Hear on the Wind." Taiwan is estimated to have about eight hundred temples dedicated to Mazu.

There are many other gods and deities in Taiwan. One popular deity is Guanyin or the Bodhisattva Avalokitesvara. A bodhisattva is an enlightened being that stays in this world to help others achieve their quest for enlightenment and nirvana. The original form of Guanyin was a male, but it evolved into a female over time because it was identified with great compassion and mercy for others. Guanyin means "She Who Looks Down and Hears the Cries of the World." Guanyin is known as the Goddess of Mercy and is one of the favorite deities for the Chinese. She is seen as a protector of women and children, as well as others in times of distress. Guanyin can be found in both Buddhist and Daoist temples.

Other deities and gods include the Jade Emperor, Guan Gong, and the Earth God. The Jade Emperor or Yuhuang, a popular god, reigns over heaven. As the supreme ruler, he has other gods reporting to him about happenings in heaven, earth, and the underworld. Guan Gong or Guanyu, sometimes known as Guandi, is the God of War. Also the God of Literature, the God of Wealth, and the God of Medicine, Guan Gong is especially liked by the Chinese, and his statue can often be found with lighted red bulbs in restaurants and stores. The Earth God or Tudigong is found everywhere in Taiwan. A representative of the Jade Emperor, he is a local god who helps the people in a community, such as farmers or storekeepers, in their problems and daily life. These deities and gods are but a few of those in the rich pantheon that exists in Chinese popular religion. A visit to Taiwan offers many opportunities to witness worship at local temples and homes. At some festivals, visitors may witness the practice of spirit mediums or *tongji* (*tang-ki*).

Christianity is still a minority religion on Taiwan. However, even though Christians are comparatively few, they are quite influential. Because of their ties to missionaries and other Christian denominations or organizations worldwide, they can draw upon a wide pool of resources and information. They have been associated with the development of schools, universities, hospitals, and orphanages. They are also a conduit for innovative ideas in Taiwan. Christians are well represented in education, government, and the social service professions.

In addition to Christianity, there are other minority religions. A number of China's ethnic minorities are Muslim. Islam was introduced to Taiwan in the seventeenth century, and its adherents mostly live in the urban areas. Many among the Taiwan aborigines who are scattered through the island practice various forms of animism.

History

Although Taiwan is only a short distance from mainland China, for many centuries Chinese did not choose to settle there. It was not that its location was unknown or that its waters were treacherous. Traders, fishermen, pirates, and others had early on discovered its shores. In fact, Taiwan was incorporated into the Chinese empire during the Tang dynasty (618–907). Nevertheless, other destinations and lands proved more attractive, providing greater opportunities for profitable returns and desirable settlements. As a result, even though some people had migrated to the western plains of Taiwan, their numbers were relatively few. During the sixteenth and seventeenth centuries, however, Chinese immigration from Fujian and Guangdong increased steadily. Fujianese, Cantonese, and the Hakka moved onto Taiwan, but the Fujianese and the Hakka were the most numerous.

In the sixteenth and seventeenth centuries, foreign contact and colonization would also occur. The Portugese encountered the "Ilha Formosa" in the early sixteenth century but did not settle there. From 1624 to 1662, the Dutch occupied a section of southwestern Taiwan and started a colony. Besides setting up forts on the island, the Dutch encouraged Chinese migration in order to promote agriculture, trade, and other economic endeavors. From 1626 to 1642, the Spanish occupied a portion of northern Taiwan as a defensive move to observe the Dutch and to protect their colony in the Philippines. However, in 1642, the Dutch attacked the Spanish and expelled them from Taiwan.

Other events in the seventeenth and eighteenth centuries drew an even greater stream of Chinese immigrants into Taiwan. The Ming dynasty

(1368–1644) was in decline and was about to give way to the Qing dynasty (1644–1911), an era in which the Chinese were to be ruled by the Manchus. The Manchus can be described as a non-Chinese people from an area northeast of China. Exploiting the divisions among the Chinese, they were able to move south of the Great Wall and eventually conquer all of China by 1683. Hoping to escape the fighting and the Manchus, some Chinese fled to Taiwan.

Taiwan became a center of Chinese resistance to the Manchus. Even after Beijing had fallen to the Manchus, Ming loyalists, supporters of the Chinese dynasty, continued to fight. Others fled to Southeast Asia. Zheng Chenggong, also known as Koxinga, continued to oppose the Manchus. He and his followers withdrew to Taiwan and in 1662 forced the Dutch to surrender and leave the island. After his death that same year, his son and grandson continued the struggle for another twenty years until the Manchus mounted a successful invasion in 1683. Taiwan then became a part of the Manchu's Chinese empire, to be administered under Fujian province. It was designated as a separate province in 1886.

During the Qing dynasty, the Chinese population in Taiwan continued to grow. After the Manchus consolidated their control, they implemented policies that gradually brought peace and prosperity to China. Agriculture also flourished, thanks to the introduction of improved production techniques and new crops such as corn (maize), potatoes, and peanuts. As a result, the Chinese population registered a dramatic increase, rising from about 150 million in 1600 to over 400 million in 1850. This expansion of the population in turn triggered large-scale population movements into China's frontier regions. People moved into Southeast China and Taiwan as well, cultivating new lands and transforming its economy. In Taiwan, the advances of the Chinese settlers led to conflicts between them and the aboriginal peoples that had to be mediated by the Qing state.

The Japanese took control of Taiwan in 1895. In the latter part of the nineteenth century, China and Japan had competed for political influence and economic position in Korea. In the resulting Sino-Japanese War of 1894 to 1895, Japan emerged victorious. In the Treaty of Shimonoseki of 1895, which brought the hostilities to an end, China was ordered to pay a large indemnity. Along with its other concessions, China agreed to cede Taiwan to Japan. For a brief time, some Chinese on the island sought autonomy and tried to create a Republic of Taiwan, but it was to no avail.

Under the Japanese occupation that lasted until 1945, Taiwan witnessed several key changes. First of all, the Japanese encouraged the improvement of agricultural production. Yields of rice, sugar, vegetables, and other crops increased. Second, they developed Taiwan's economic infrastructure by emphasizing transportation and communication. A system of railroads was expanded, roads were constructed and harbors built. The Japanese provided inexpensive hydroelectric power, enabling small industry to grow and commerce to flourish. Moreover, disease was eradicated, and a focus on public hygiene bettered the living conditions and health of the people. Finally, they erected an elaborate system of colonial education for learning at the school, college, and university levels. It was a system that promoted literacy in Japanese and professional education in practical specialties such as engineering, technology, science, agriculture, and medicine.

With Japan's defeat at the end of World War II in 1945, Taiwan was returned to China. Unfortunately, conflict soon broke out between the mainlanders and the Taiwanese. As they took over control from the Japanese, mainland Chinese officials and soldiers were insensitive to the feelings of the local population. Some of them looked down upon a population that spoke a different dialect and that had been under Japanese rule for fifty years. On February 28, 1947, the killing of a Taiwanese by police led to an angry reaction, civil disorder, and rebellion. Reprisals by the government followed. By the time the event had run its course, several thousand Taiwanese had been killed. The episode alienated the Taiwanese and widened the gulf between them and the mainlanders. The February 28 Incident or *er er ba* (literally, "2–28") thenceforth became a reference point in talking about the history of Taiwan.

Meanwhile, on the mainland of China, civil war broke out between the Nationalist government and the Communists. In this epic struggle, the Communists swept the Nationalists before them. As the Communists marched into Beijing and proclaimed a new People's Republic of China, the Nationalists were forced to retreat to Taiwan. Between one to two million officials, soldiers, and civilians from the mainland fled to the island. They joined the estimated six million Taiwanese already there. Under their leader Jiang Jieshi (Chiang Kai-shek), the Nationalists maintained a Republic of China on Taiwan with Taibei as its capital.

Although the Republic of China had been pushed off the mainland, the United States recognized it as the legitimate government for China. For their part, the Chinese Communists made preparations to invade Taiwan so that they could complete their conquest of China. However, the outbreak of the Korean War in 1950 thwarted their goal. U.S. President Harry Truman decided to order the Seventh Fleet into the Taiwan Strait to protect the island from any Communist attacks. For thirty more years, Washington ignored mainland China and acknowledged only Taibei as the official government of China.

Restricted to Taiwan, the Nationalist government continued to maintain that it was the legitimate government for all of China and imposed the governmental structure of the Republic of China on the provincial government of Taiwan. Mainlanders continued to serve without elections in the National Assembly and the Legislative Yuan to represent all the different provinces of China on the mainland. In this fashion, the form and appearance of a national government for the mainland was perpetuated on Taiwan.

Nonetheless, by the 1970s, more governments around the world recognized the People's Republic of China with its capital in Beijing. In 1971, mainland China was admitted to the United Nations, and the Republic of China was ousted. In the following year, President Richard Nixon visited China and, with his national security adviser Henry Kissinger, arranged for the United States to normalize relations with Beijing. The Shanghai Communique affirmed the views of Beijing and Taiwan that there was only one China and that Taiwan was a part of it. Several years later, in 1979, President Jimmy Carter severed relations with Taiwan and formally recognized the People's Republic of China. By the 1980s, only about twenty countries recognized the Republic of China, although many others maintained informal contact for trade and commerce.

While shunned by most of the world, Taiwan had positioned itself as a major economic power on the world scene. Initially seen as a producer of cheap goods and inexpensive electronic items, by the 1980s Taiwan boasted one of the highest per capita income levels in Asia along with Japan and Hong Kong, and economic pundits spoke of it as one of the "four young tigers" or "four young dragons." Comprised of Hong Kong, Taiwan, South Korea, and Singapore, these were dynamic economies that were transforming the Asian-Pacific region into a global center for international trade.

Important political changes also began to take place on Taiwan. Since 1949, Taiwan had been under martial law, partly as a response to the Chinese civil war but also partly to facilitate mainlander and Nationalist Party control over the island. When Jiang Jieshi died in 1975, his son Jiang Jingguo (Chiang Ching-kuo) succeeded him. The younger Jiang ended martial law in 1987 and adopted measures to bring more Taiwanese into the Nationalist Party, the government, and the military. He selected Li Denghui (Lee Teng-hui), a Taiwanese, to be his vice-president.

When Jiang Jingguo died in 1988, Li succeeded him to become the first Taiwanese president. Li appointed Lian Zhan (Lien Chan), also a Taiwanese, to be the premier of Taiwan. Under Presidents Jiang Jingguo and Li Denghui, Taiwan's one-party system of government moved toward greater openness and democracy. Political parties opposing the ruling Nationalist Party were allowed to organize in 1986. In 1991, democratic elections were permitted for the National Assembly. A few years later, in 1996, in the first ever popular election for the president of Taiwan, Li was elected with 54 percent of the votes cast. In short, the political reforms that had been introduced since the 1980s seemed to herald further changes and promise a larger voice for the people of Taiwan.

2

Coming to America

IMMIGRATION

Early Chinese Immigration

Substantial Chinese immigration preceded that of the Taiwanese by more than a century. In the mid-nineteenth century, large numbers of Cantonese from the mainland province of Guangdong came to the West Coast in search of work. The discovery of gold in California made them aware of the opportunities in the United States. In their quest for employment, they engaged in mining, the building of railroads, agriculture, fishing, industry, gardening, and domestic service. In agriculture, they not only farmed but also helped in land reclamation by draining swamps and marshes. In areas that were dry and less well watered, they helped to dig irrigation ditches and canals. In addition, they also opened small businesses such as restaurants and laundries. The work done by these earlier Chinese pioneers helped to develop the American West and to pave the way for the expansion of the American economy.

The increasing presence of the Chinese in the United States eventually triggered an anti-Chinese movement, however. Fueled by labor unions that resented the competition of foreign labor, the movement drew strength from those who subscribed to nativism, xenophobia, and racism. It led to discriminatory local and state statutes, school segregation, antimiscegenation laws, even violence, and picking up momentum, it resulted in the passage of an exclusion act against the Chinese in 1882. The legislation had the dubious distinction of being the first to deny people from another country entry to the United States because of their ancestry or ethnicity. Prior to this event, only the criminal, diseased, or mentally ill had been refused admission.

Because the legislation was such a novel departure from the country's previous policy of open door immigration, it was framed to be effective for only ten years. This was a tactic to secure passage in the Congress. But in 1892 and 1902, the legislation was repeatedly renewed for ten-year periods. Finally, in 1904, the legislation was made permanent. The result was to deny Chinese entry to the United States until World War II. First-generation Chinese who were born outside of the United States were also denied the right to naturalize for American citizenship.

In the years after 1882, the Chinese essentially lived in the shadow of exclusion. Denied the opportunity to be U.S. citizens, they lived on the margins of American society. In 1910, the Chinese who immigrated into the United States were sent to Angel Island in San Francisco Bay, where they had to face detailed interrogation. Partly because officials reflected the attitudes embodied in the exclusion laws, the Chinese were subjected to especially close investigation. Nonetheless, the great San Francisco earthquake and fire of 1906 had destroyed many immigration records and opened the way for "paper son immigration." A "paper son" was one who was allegedly born when a Chinese resident of the United States returned home and had children. These children were then entitled to return to the United States.

Suspicious of deception, U.S. immigration officials at Angel Island often viewed the Chinese as adversaries. They questioned the potential immigrants about minutiae regarding their residences, villages, relatives, and acquaintances. Thus, a person might be asked how many people lived in a house nearby or in an alley. The description of the facade or interior of a home might also be sought. If people's memories failed them, they might be rejected and sent back to China. As a result, many Chinese saw Angel Island as being more a site of prejudice and discrimination than an immigration station. On the walls of the station that housed them, they inscribed poems lamenting their confinement and their uncertain fate.

Angel Island continued to be used as an immigration station for the Chinese and other Asians, such as the Japanese, until 1940. In recent years, some of the Chinese poems written on the site have been collected, translated, and published. (Lai, Lim, and Yung 1980). The site of the former immigration station has also been recognized as an important historical site for many Chinese and Asians. They view it as the "Ellis Island of the West," and tours are conducted on Angel Island to acquaint people with its significance in Asian American history.

During World War II, however, China became an ally of the United States in joint efforts to defeat Japan. During this period, editor Richard Walsh and his wife, the noted author Pearl Buck, and others spearheaded efforts to end the exclusionary laws against China. They argued that on both moral and practical war-related grounds, the United States should lift the tradition of Chinese exclusion that had been in force since 1882. With the support of President Franklin Roosevelt, the repeal of the Chinese Exclusion Act became a reality in 1943. A quota of one hundred five Chinese persons were permitted to enter each year. Moreover, first-generation Chinese were now granted the right to naturalize for American citizenship. In the subsequent War Brides Act of 1945 and Fiancees Act of 1946, some Chinese were admitted. The Displaced Persons Act of 1948 and the Refugee Relief Act of 1953 also allowed some Chinese refugees from the Chinese civil war between the Nationalists and the Communists to enter the United States.

Taiwanese Immigration

In 1965, President Lyndon B. Johnson signed the Hart-Celler Act, also known as the Immigration and Nationality Act of 1965. Signed at the foot of the Statue of Liberty at Ellis Island, the bill sought to give more balanced immigration to Asians. It allowed for family reunification, tried to reduce the large backlog of those who were waiting for admission and to correct a legacy of anti-Asian bias in the nation's immigration laws.

The Immigration Act of 1965 was important, for it allowed more Chinese to enter the country. Unlike the McCarran-Walter Act of 1952 which allotted a token quota of one hundred Chinese, the new legislation permitted an annual quota of twenty thousand. At the same time, others could come in as nonquota immigrants if they were spouses, unmarried minor children, or the parents of U.S. citizens. Chinese immigration, along with that from the Philippines, India, and South Korea, would rise substantially after 1965.

Immigration from Taiwan can be divided into three periods. One is from after World War II to 1965. During this period, a small number of students scattered throughout the United States. Having completed their military service in Taiwan, they then left home for further study in this country. They were not particularly well off, but they saw that coming to the United States was a continuation of the trend of previous Chinese who had trained in this country. Starting in 1954, the Taiwan government administered annual examinations for those who wished to study abroad to determine if they had fulfilled their military service. This screening process would end in 1976.

For veterans of this era, the favored places were along the West Coast or the East Coast. Others congregated in the Midwest in places such as Chicago.

Hoping to save on spending and also craving companionship, many roomed together in apartments. They often shared buying, cooking, and mealtimes. During the week, they were busy with classes and studies. On weekends, they might visit the local Chinatown for groceries and perhaps a meal at a nearby Chinese restaurant. During the winter months in the Midwest or the East Coast, they gathered to socialize in apartments warmed by radiators. On the whole, their numbers were relatively few. Among the Chinese in the United States, there still were not many speakers of Mandarin, except for emigré refugees and former officials from Nationalist China. Otherwise, they were awash in a community of Cantonese speakers, most of whom spoke a Siyi or Taishan dialect. After their studies, many hoped to find jobs in the United States.

There were also some people from Taiwan, who were married to American service personnel. For the most part, they were Chinese women married to U.S. soldiers who had been stationed in Taiwan, particularly after the Korean War. That conflict and the Cold War had led to the signing of a Mutual Defense Treaty in 1954, in which the United States pledged to protect the safety of Taiwan. As a result, there was a noticeable American presence on Taiwan. When these service personnel returned to the United States, their Chinese spouses accompanied them. In some cases, these members of the military were Chinese Americans who brought back Chinese wives.

Finally, there were others who came to work. They saw economic conditions in the United States as being much more favorable. Regardless of the kind of work they might do, the pay seemed much better than in Taiwan. Some toiled in Chinese restaurants, while others found jobs in the service sector. But the appeal of America was great, and some even jumped ship to land in the United States.

The second period dates from 1965 to 1979. The Immigration Act of 1965 increased the quota of Chinese immigrants to twenty thousand. There was a provision for family reunification that was not restricted by any quota numbers. This tended to help those who were of Cantonese background. They had the opportunity to bring family members—wives, parents, or children—who had been waiting on long lists because of the small number permitted in the 1943 Act. This family reunification provision initially helped only a few immigrants from Taiwan, as not many had settled in this country as yet.

But the same bill also had a system of preferences. There was a preference specifying that persons who possessed vital and exceptional skills could be permitted to immigrate to the United States. Thus, those who had important technical and scientific skills in critical areas could secure entry and employment. Yet at the same time, those who might be in needed occupations, such as cooks, restaurant chefs, and so on might also secure admittance. A fair number from Taiwan were in this way to gain admission to the United States through these preference categories.

The third period begins in 1979 and continues to the present day. In 1979, the United States established formal diplomatic relations with the People's Republic of China and broke off relations with Taiwan, or the Republic of China. In the Shanghai Communique of 1972, the United States recognized only one China. By setting up an embassy in Beijing, it indicated implicitly that that one was mainland China. As a result, the quota of twenty thousand was shared between China and Taiwan.

Without any formal U.S. ties to Taibei, diplomatic relations between the United States and Taiwan took on a different face and were maintained through informal mechanisms. Since the United States no longer recognized Taiwan, no embassy could be established in Taibei. Nor could Taiwan establish an embassy in Washington, D.C. Instead, an American Institute in Taiwan (AIT) was created, which was staffed by U.S. State Department personnel. It assumed the responsibility of an informal embassy, essentially discharging all the functions of an embassy or a consulate and watched out for U.S. political and commercial interests in Taiwan. Having a similar role was the Coordination Council for North American Affairs (CCNAA). It, too, operated as an informal embassy with a few regional offices similar to consulates and handled similar political and economic responsibilities.

For those coming in from Taiwan during this period, it was almost as if they were nonpersons. They read that in the U.S. capital,Washington, D.C., officials from the Republic of China could not attend formal diplomatic functions. All across the United States the flag of the Republic of China (*qingtian bairi mandihong qi*) was removed from flag displays at schools and convention centers. In its place was displayed the flag of the People's Republic of China (*wuxing hongqi*). This was a consequence of the nonrecognized status of the Republic of China. As a result, they were people from an "invisible country," or a province of the People's Republic of China. There were stories of international difficulties and indignities in holding passports from a country "that did not exist." Facing these shocks, many from Taiwan were hurt and humiliated. At student and community gatherings, there were emotional, tear-filled renderings of the song "*Meihua*" (Plum Blossom), a flower symbolizing the Republic of China. On occasion, they also sang "*Zhonghua Minguo Song*," a song whose title can be translated as "The Republic of China Hymn." Taiwan, it seemed, was now hidden in the shadow of China.

However, in 1982, the United States decided to offer Taiwan a quota of twenty thousand persons. The earlier Taiwan Relations Act of 1979 had stated that Taiwan could receive an immigration quota as if it were a separate state. The new legislation, which had been passed in 1981 to be effective in 1982, immediately aroused protest from Beijing. It argued that the assignment of a separate quota to Taiwan signified that the Republic of China was a separate country, apart from mainland China. American officials denied that that was their intent. Rather, they declared that the new quota would help reduce the backlog of people hoping to immigrate into the United States from Taiwan and China under the single twenty thousand quota. People on the list of hopefuls had been looking at waiting periods of five to six years. In the early 1980s, resident Chinese from Taiwan were numerous enough to sponsor relatives. Thus, a chain migration of Taiwan immigrants was developing and causing quite a backlist of those who sought entry.

By this time, the motives for emigration to the United States had changed as well. In addition to the previous goal of studying in the United States, now others sought the economic opportunity in the United States. Taiwan was training more students to be professionals, even as those trained in the United States could not easily find jobs in their homeland. Taiwan was in the situation of many developing countries where jobs lagged behind the growth of a professionally trained class. As a result, students trained in both Taiwan and the United States sought employment in the United States— especially those who had studied in this country, were accustomed to its way of life, and found it rather congenial to their expectations. Already used to well-equipped U.S. science laboratories or research facilities with expensive equipment, many did not wish to go back to Taiwan, which did not offer comparable support.

The numbers of students who came to the United States to stay was high. In a sense, they constituted a "brain drain" of human capital from Taiwan, where they had already received a strong high school and college education. Subject to a draft in Taiwan, males could study abroad upon completion of their military service. After receiving their graduate education in the United States, they simply found jobs here instead of returning home.

An Immigration Act of 1990 revised the system of preferences established in the 1965 Act. However, it included employment-based preferences for those with key professional, research, and occupational skills. Thus professionals, executives, those with advanced degrees, and others were eligible for admission. Another category included investors who could create employment. Wealthy businessmen in Taiwan could apply for immigration if they were willing to invest funds to start a business. In fact, the Immigration Act of 1990 made it easier for investors to move into the United States, and many from Taiwan took advantage of this provision.

Another consideration was for the education of their children. There are only so many opportunities for the education of the youth in Taiwan. Taiwan has a limited number of universities, and its people have long valued education at the university and college level. The national examinations to gain admittance are extremely competitive and are seen as the ticket to a successful, professional life. High school students take the examinations as a body, and the scores are eventually posted so that people can learn the outcome. Because of the intense competition, parents often send their children to cram schools to enhance their preparedness.

In comparison, the United States has an abundance of public and private universities and colleges. The competition is not as stiff in all the universities, and higher education is more readily available to all. Knowing the accessibility of American higher education and the prestige of the American system of universities internationally, parents in Taiwan have immigrated with their children in mind. Many feel that Taiwan is like an "examination hell" for their children. In contrast, the United States is more humane and relaxed. Moreover, their children will be able to lead more normal, balanced lives without anxieties about admission to a university after high school.

Furthermore, there was the matter of Taiwan's uncertain fate. In 1979, derecognition of the Republic of China by the United States and the termination of the Mutual Defense Act between the two caused many to fear that China might move to unify the island with the mainland. Although the Shanghai Communique stated that the United States would sell arms to Taiwan to maintain its defenses, there were fears about Taiwan's ability to maintain its independence in the face of a determined mainland China. Anxious about what might happen were that the case, Taiwanese began to move capital abroad. Simultaneously, they sought to immigrate to the United States.

By the mid-1980s, Taiwan had achieved prominence as an economic miracle, a major economic power. With abundant capital, businessmen in Taiwan sought to invest in the United States. Those who had immigrated to the United States now saw that there were opportunities to participate in both the Taiwan and U.S. sides of the Pacific Rim economy. Whether as representatives of U.S. corporations in Taiwan or going back to work in Taiwan, these transnational Taiwanese called *taikongren* or "astronauts" freely moved back and forth across the Pacific. Some left their wives and children in the United States while they worked in Taiwan. Others worked

with their wives in Taiwan but left their children in the United States. Some
were simply homesick and valued life in Taiwan more but wanted educational
opportunities for their children. These "parachute children" or *xiao xialiu
xuesheng*, translated literally as "little students abroad," are left in the hands
of caretakers. These may be relatives or friends. Or, they may live by themselves in a house that has been bought by their parents.

As the numbers of immigrants from Taiwan have increased, they have set
up networks to help one another. In academia, for example, one can discern
networks among different groups of Chinese. One network is made up of
the Chinese from Taiwan. Until recently, in fields like Chinese studies, many
were able to secure positions in American universities and colleges. But since
the normalization of U.S. relations with Beijing, many such positions are
now going to people from China. A competing network of those from mainland China now exists, and one can readily discern this by noting the names
using the pinyin romanization system with X's and Q's. Other networks that
may be noticed are made up of Chinese from Hong Kong and those from
Singapore and Malaysia.

Composition of New Immigrants

New immigrants arriving from Taiwan today present a contrast to the
Chinese immigrants before 1965. They are more likely to have a higher level
of education than other Chinese immigrants. In fact, their educational level
is higher than that of immigrants from Hong Kong, and even more than
that of immigrants from China. On the other hand, those from Hong Kong
are more likely to have a better command of English, even as those from
Taiwan have a higher level of fluency in English than those from China.

The educational attainment of immigrants from Taiwan reflects a familiarity with the American educational system. Since World War II, the intimate relationship between the United States and Taiwan led to many
educational and cultural exchanges between the two areas. Those who received graduate training and returned to Taiwan began to reorganize its
educational programs according to the American model. This occurred despite the warnings of some critics that it meant that it was neglecting alternative models in other European countries or the example of Japan in Asia.

The close ties that had been fostered led to a continuous flow of Taiwan
students into American universities. It also meant that the prestige of the
U.S. model has been widely publicized, so that many students yearn to study
abroad in America. Once in the United States, many accept positions—
adding to the "brain drain." As a result, the government of Taiwan has

moved to develop a more extensive offering of doctoral level graduate programs so that students can be kept at home. In recent years, leaders from Taiwan have also tried to entice professionals, scientists, professors, researchers, and others to return. And undoubtedly this can be attractive to those who wish to go back to the land of their birth. This is especially so since Taiwan can now afford to pay very competitive salaries.

Whether this strategy by Taiwan will be successful remains to be seen. But it does mean that the skill level of the immigrants from Taiwan is quite high because of the Taiwanese emphasis on science, mathematics, engineering, technology, and computer science. This background also gives business executives and experienced entrepreneurs who have seen the opportunity for expansion in the United States a good chance to do well in the American labor market.

Whereas in Chinese immigration before World War II, the composition was predominantly male, today females constitute the majority. Like their male counterparts, many of them seek educational opportunity in this country. Also, a second phase of migration from Taiwan, the chain migration of family members, has led to a more diversified community, for it is now not only professionals who can came to America. It also needs to be noted that not all immigrants from Taiwan are a model minority of engineers, technicians, and computer scientists. Since the early Taiwanese immigration, there have also been blue collar workers, manual laborers, cooks, and garment seamstresses.

The large influx of immigrants from Taiwan since 1965 has led to a noticeable Taiwanese presence in the United States. There are large communities scattered throughout the different sections of the country. For example, large numbers of Taiwanese Americans have congregated in California because of its favorable climate and hospitable economic environment. In the northern part of the state, many have found employment in the San Jose and Silicon Valley area. In Southern California, many have concentrated in the greater Los Angeles area. The city of Monterey Park, which has been described as the first suburban Chinatown, has also been called "Little Taibei" (Fong 1994:vii; Horton 1995:37). Many Taiwanese have settled in other suburban communities that are seen as relatively affluent middle class neighborhoods throughout the San Gabriel valley.

In the East, a sizable community of Taiwanese can now be found in the Queens-Flushing area of New York (H. Chen 1992). In Texas, Houston also has a fast-growing population of Taiwanese. But while the communities in California, New York, and Texas receive much of the attention, many Taiwanese have settled in other areas throughout the United States—in New

Chinese characters indicate the site of a hospital in Monterey Park, California. Courtesy of Polly Lo.

Jersey, Illinois, Washington, and many other states. For the Taiwanese, it is not necessary to locate in an older, urban Chinatown. Many have dispersed throughout the cities and towns of the United States. If they have a business in a Chinatown in San Francisco, New York, Los Angeles, or Houston, they are likely to have homes elsewhere.

The entry of Taiwanese to the United States is more than just a flow of immigrants. Economists would label them human capital, noting that they are trained and educated labor that can benefit the American economy. With their arrival, there is also a capital flow and a culture flow. The capital flow refers to the economic strength of Taiwan due to its remarkable transformation in the past two decades. Taiwanese immigrants and entrepreneurs see the United States as a secure site for investment and business opportunities. They have started up new ventures and revitalized decaying or slumbering communities. At the same time, the culture flow is the knowledge, information, and culture that the immigrants bring with them. Simultaneously both are making an impact and altering the economic and cultural landscape of America.

California stands as a good example of the Taiwanese effect on the U.S. cultural landscape. Whether in San Jose or in Los Angeles, the Taiwanese presence is evident. Shopping malls or strip malls appear as Chinese oases,

A Taiwanese shopping center in Southern California. Courtesy of Polly Lo.

almost as if they were transplanted from Taiwan or Hong Kong. Chinese restaurants are everywhere with signs offering Taiwanese and other Chinese regional cuisines. There are also Islamic Chinese restaurants with fresh breads, lamb dishes, and vegetable dumplings. There are even Japanese restaurants opened by the Taiwanese, who are familiar with such cuisine because of the Japanese occupation of Taiwan from 1895 to 1945. These restaurants often display the *maneki-neko* or "beckoning cat," a Japanese talisman for good luck and good fortune. Refreshments such as soybean milk drinks and red bean floats with ice cream are on all the menus. Large Asian supermarkets offer Asian and Chinese fruits and vegetables such as pomelos, starfruit, lichee, dragon eyes, Chinese stringbeans, Chinese broccoli, and so on.

A casual stroll on San Gabriel Boulevard reveals Chinese and Taiwanese real estate companies, banks, groceries, automobile dealers, and pharmacies. Advertisements everywhere appeal to consumers to get a cellular phone or to sign up so that they can call friends and relatives in Taiwan, China, or Hong Kong. Newstands offer competing Chinese daily newspapers, several of which are branches of those in Taiwan. Videostores, karaoke clubs, and travel companies seem to crowd the landscape. The Chinese characters are intermingled with English words, a kind of bilingualism that may be disconcerting to the uninitiated. To find a translation service or to have a photograph taken for

A supermarket stocks bitter melon, a food item popular with the Taiwanese. Courtesy of Polly Lo.

a passport, one need only consult the *Asian Yellow Pages*. The *Asian Yellow Pages*, telephone directories with advertisements, can be found in many communities with Chinese and Taiwanese. If the population is large, the directories can be in both Chinese and English. In some cities, there are also *Asian Yellow Pages* directories for the diverse Asian American population.

But even in communities with smaller populations of Taiwanese Americans, active networks may exist. Geographical concentration or density of population is not necessary for an ethnic community to develop. It is true that places like Monterey Park and San Jose have stronger semblances to institutional completeness—the presence of associations, newspapers, churches, enterprises, and other community organizations. Thanks to the wonders of modern communication and technology, E-mail, the Internet, satellite television, cable channels, cellular phones, and videotapes, there can be a circuitry that ties Taiwanese Americans with others in the same locale or with those elsewhere in the United States or Taiwan.

FAMILY

The family was the building block of traditional Chinese society. Much of this was due to Confucian values, which tended to place a premium on

Refrigerated areas feature fish cake, fish balls, and condiments used in preparing Taiwanese dishes. Courtesy of Polly Lo.

the importance of family. As a result, in traditional China, clans and lineages were significant factors in local politics. They could mobilize resources, financial or human labor as the situation demanded. They could provide tutors or an education for the gifted children of the clan. On the whole, those clans and lineages in Southern China were more extensive and complete than those in the north.

Confucian values are associated with the five relationships that specify the important ties that maintain a family and society. The first is of subject and ruler: the subject is to obey the ruler. The second is of the father to the son: the son is to obey the father. The third is of the wife to the husband: the wife is to be obedient to her husband. The fourth is of the younger brother to the older brother: the younger brother should obey the older brother. Finally, in the fifth, a friend should respect a friend.

According to some interpreters of Confucian values, of the five relationships, three pertain to the family. Moreover, it has been noticed that of the five bonds, four are from the top down. That is, one of the two in each dyad is subordinate, while the other is dominant. Some scholars explain, however, that the five bonds are not to subjugate. Rather they claim that there must be reciprocal responsibility. A ruler to merit being called a ruler must take care of his subjects. To win respect from his son a father must deport himself as a father. To keep his wife a husband must be solicitous of her needs. A younger brother is expected to defer or learn from the experience of his older brother, but the older brother must be aware of what he is doing wrong. Finally, a friend must reciprocate acts by his friend to maintain the tie.

The Status of Family Members

Traditional family values placed an emphasis on the continuity of the family name. The family was patrilineal in the sense that the male line continued through the sons. For this reason, having sons was stressed: they could ensure the duration of the family line. Sons could carry on the rites to respect the ancestors. In fact, in the rites to commemorate ancestors, only males could conduct the ceremonies.

Also, in an agricultural society, having many sons meant that there would be a larger reservoir of labor to help in the fields. In other endeavors, it meant that there might be more to help in the family business. Finally, sons could be deployed to diversify the family's resources and to enhance the family's economic and social status. A very talented son, for example, might be schooled to master the classics for the imperial examinations. Success in the examinations might lead to appointment to a post in the imperial bureaucracy, thereby conferring prestige and power to the family.

The family was hierarchical and respected seniority. A generation should respect the generations above it. Thus, a father should respect his own father; a grandson, his grandfather. A younger brother should respect the older brother; a younger sister, the older one. Those who were older had the benefit of greater experience and wisdom and should therefore be heeded.

Women who married were seen as marrying out of the family. They were marrying into another family and were to bear children for that family. In her new home, the new wife was expected to help out with the chores and to assist the mother of her husband. When she bore a son, her status in the family was elevated, for she had born another male who could carry on the name of her husband's family.

Chinese society was considered patriarchal as men held the formal authority in the family. The position of women was noted in the "three obediences." According to this perspective, when a woman was young, she obeyed her father. When she was married, she obeyed her husband. And, when she was a widow, she obeyed her son. This is not to say, however, that women did not have informal power.

Children were seen as the raison d'etre for the family. In traditional China, an abundance of children was seen as a blessing. It suggested a prosperous and lucky household, with many members to assure the biological continuity and the economic success of the family. Of course, having many children was only desirable if the family had the means to support them. Otherwise, there would be problems in feeding so many mouths. Children were also a form of insurance to support parents in their old age in a society where there was no assurance of financial security or assistance upon retirement from work.

Among the families of those from Taiwan, the number of children is not as great as in the past. As in countries that are developed and industrial, couples elect not to have as many offspring as it is not as necessary for the economic security of the family. Taiwanese American families in the United States are nuclear families similar to those of other Chinese Americans.

Changes in Taiwan and the United States

In recent years, Taiwan has become much more urban and industrialized, so much so that it is now a major economic power in the world. This change in its economic status has also had effects upon its society and its families. With a population of 21.53 million in 1996, Taiwan had 0.4 of the world's total population. It had 6.02 million households, with an average of 3.57 persons in each. In the ratio of males to females, there were 106 males to every 100 females. The imbalance reflects a traditional preference for males in Chinese culture. Because of this imbalance, the newspapers and media occasionally reported the securing of Chinese brides from mainland China.

Marriages occurred at a later age. Men were marrying at an average of 31.6 years of age, while the average for women was at 29.5 years of age. More than 169,000 couples were married in Taiwan in 1996. In the same year, there were 35,800 divorces, indicating that this practice was on the rise. Demographic statistics revealed that there was an average of 1.77 children for each woman. Children born out of wedlock were recorded at 2.84 percent for all births in 1996. The number of single parent households increased to 380,000 in Taiwan, amounting to 6.6 percent of all the families. This reflected the increases in divorce rates and the number of unwed mothers. Of these single parent households, 70 percent of them were headed by women (Sheng 1997:4).

In the United States, family is also an important theme for the Taiwanese. The ideal family was traditionally envisioned to be an extended family. This might be a family with three generations under one roof—grandparents, their children and their wives, and their grandchildren. Or, it might be a joint family, including two brothers, their wives, and their children. Particularly in a traditional society that emphasized agriculture, a large family in one household was considered a benefit.

In the United States, the extended family may be found, but it often is the nuclear family. In Taiwan, important economic changes have de-emphasized the need for large families as was required in agriculture. With movement from rural to urban areas, many are now employed in sectors other than farming. Changes bringing prosperity to Taiwan society also mitigate the need for many sons to take care of the security of parents after their retirement.

In the United States, there are even fewer extended families. Couples migrating to America often have left their parents and siblings behind in Taiwan. As a result, they live by themselves even as their parents continue to reside in Taiwan. But they try to maintain relations with their parents by constantly phoning back home to Taiwan. Moreover, if the circumstances permit, there may be occasional trips to visit parents and relatives. As a result, even though there may be physical separation, an emotional intimacy bridges the gulf in distance.

In some households, other relatives may live with the nuclear family comprised of the parents and their children. For example, a sister's family may be residing in the Midwest of the United States. But the other sister lives on the West Coast in California. The nephew from the Midwest may live with the aunt and uncle on the West Coast as he attends a university in the neighborhood in which they live. This is a way of conserving financial resources and also insuring that the nephew even at college will be under the careful guidance of family members. It is also a way of rekindling familial relationships.

Within a household of a first-generation family from Taiwan, Chinese kinship terminology is likely to be used. This type of family terminology is much more specific and precise than that of the general American society. Thus, the words for grandparents will denote whether they are the relations of the father or the mother. *Zufumu* is the term for parents of one's father, while *waizufumu* is the term for parents of one's mother. Or, the words for brother and sister will denote their rank and seniority, whether they are younger or older than the speaker. *Gege* is the term for an older brother, while *didi* is the term for a younger brother. *Jiejie* is the term for an older sister; *meimei*, for a younger sister.

In the case of terms for uncles and aunts, there will be embedded in the words the indication of whether they are from the father or mother's side, and their rank or seniority as the oldest uncle or youngest aunt as well. *Bofu* is the older brother of one's father, while *shufu* is the father's younger brother. *Jiufu* is the brother of one's mother. *Bofu, zufu,* and *jiufu* in the United States are simply referred to as "uncles." *Gumu* is the sister of one's father; *yimu,* the sister of one's mother. In the United States, both *gumu* and *yimu* are simply referred to as "aunts." In the case of cousins, the terms used will signify whether they are older or younger and whether they come from the father or mother's family.

Often a family in which there is a second generation will not be as precise in their use of the kinship terminology. Not as familiar with the Chinese or Taiwanese language, they may have trouble keeping track of the precise usage of the terms for relatives. The more acculturated they are, the more likely they are to adopt the more generalized American kinship terminology of just saying "aunt" or "uncle," which do not recognize their link to the father or mother's side of the relatives or their rank in terms of age or seniority.

In the United States, family relations are modified compared to the situation in Taiwan. In the United States, the situation may vary according to the economic situation of the families. Broadly speaking, it may be said that there are two kinds of families. One would be the Chinatown family of those who are employed by others, often in a Chinatown or urban area. The members of such a family would often be working class, laboring in a garment factory, restaurant, or tourist shop, in manufacturing, service, or some other small business.

For those in this scenario, the hours may be long and the wages not that high. In a garment factory, the women sit poised before their machines, sewing or assembling the clothing that must be conveyed from the subcontractors to the larger outlets or department stores. In a restaurant, the waiters, cooks, and busboys must contend with long hours and a wide variety of chores. Competition is fierce, and the flow of customers when it comes is fast and frenetic. In the tourist and curio shops, success is dependent on the economy and the tourist traffic. High rents dictate that there must be a sizable volume of windowshoppers and tourists, or else the businesses will not be able to recoup their costs of operation.

Typically there are two wage earners as their income is not in a high range. For this reason, the male and the female may be coequal breadwinners as they both have an important role to play in securing income for the family. In such a situation, the husband and wife may not see each other frequently. Children may be left to fend for themselves, with perhaps the oldest ones entrusted to take care of the younger siblings. If it is an extended family, the grandparents may help in the care of the younger children.

A beauty salon advertises Taiwanese-style hair-
cuts. Courtesy of Polly Lo.

In such a family, the roles may be much more traditional. The father may
have a stronger, more dominant status. His opinions are more likely to carry
weight, and the mother may echo his views. Because of their heavy involvement with work, they may not have much time with their children. As a
result, there may be misunderstanding, a lack of communication, and even
a widened generation gap between the parents and their children who are
much more acculturated.

Another type of family is the professional family. In this type of family,
the couple are usually of the middle class and engaged in white-collar employment. They have a college level education and perhaps postgraduate as
well from Taiwan or the United States. They might be accountants, engineers, computer scientists, insurance agents, or financial managers. With this
type of employment, the family enjoys a high level of income and a respect-

able social status. Their homes may be in suburban areas or in urban neighborhoods away from Chinatowns.

For the professional family, the relations between the husband and wife are more egalitarian. They are more acquainted with middle-class mores and are more acculturated than their Chinatown or working-class counterparts. Their lifestyle affords them more leisure and time for recreation. It also means that they may spend more time with their children, participating in their school and extracurricular activities. They are more able to participate in community activities and to network with others in the Chinese or non-Chinese community.

Values and Customs

The families of immigrants from Taiwan, regardless of whether they are of the working or professional class, are likely to emphasize traditional Chinese values to their children. Although there may be a diversity in the degree of practice, the ideals are nonetheless common to many of these families. The ideals are likely to focus on the significance of family, filial piety, and respect for elders,

Children are told from an early age that the family is important. In Taiwanese society, an individual is nothing unless he or she is affiliated with a group. Of these groups, the family assumes paramount significance. But the family is not merely the nuclear family. It also extends to relatives beyond the nuclear family to those on the father's and mother's side. Kinship ties form a vast network that can help in many situations, so children are urged to always value relatives.

The children are hardly likely to forget that they are part of a family. In most cases they are given another name besides their English name. The Chinese or Taiwanese name usually consists of three words or characters, although in a few instances there may be two words or characters. The traditional way of listing a person's name was to give first the family surname and then the individual's name. As an illustration, for Li Dayi, Li would be the family name and Dayi is the person's name. But in the United States, the practice is to list the surname last. So if one only had a Chinese name, he is called Dayi Li. If he had both an English and a Chinese name, he might be identified as David Dayi Li or Dayi David Li.

One of the values that the parents are likely to pass on to their children is the importance of filial piety. Parents are the ones who are endowed with more experience and wisdom. They bring food to the table, shelter the children, and have made the sacrifice of coming to the United States so that the family could have a better life. Above all, they have brought the children into this world and have nurtured them.

For this reason, the children are obligated to obey their parents. The obligation of children to parents is one that can never be repaid. Their duties and responsibilities are to try to satisfy their parents by doing well in school, and to excel in their endeavors so as to bring honor to the family name. Older siblings should try to watch and help their younger brothers and sisters, and finally, they should try to avoid conflict with one another. As a family, they should try to be a cohesive and harmonious unit.

Children are taught how to deport themselves. That means that in the presence of family members, adults, and those in authority, children should observe proper etiquette and demonstrate correct manners. Children are warned that people can easily distinguish between those who have good breeding and teaching and those who do not. When in the public gaze, when at the meal table, or whatever setting it might be, children should always conduct themselves properly with appropriate propriety and decorum.

Another important value for the children that parents emphasize is the importance of education. This theme is consistent with Confucian values, and the parents have no problem in conveying it. They may mention how Taiwan used to be a developing country. They may emphasize that education helped in the transformation of Taiwan. They may also talk about how difficult it is to secure entry into one of Taiwan's prestigious universities. In the United States, the competition is much less fierce, but the children should still try their best to get into a prestigious college or university. One important change is that whereas in the past a high level of education was not seen as necessary or even desirable for a woman, that is no longer the case.

A great deal of emphasis is placed on success in achievement or accomplishment. Children are enjoined to strive to do well in whatever field of endeavor they enter. Whether it be a public or private career, whether it be education or extracurricular activities, they should try to do their best. The obverse side of this is that individuals should not bring shame or dishonor to the family. One should be aware that whatever is done will reflect upon the parents and others who are associated with that person. When there is success, it bestows prestige on the family. But when something brings shame or the loss of face, it hurts the family and those linked to that individual.

A person or a family encounters different stages through life. Marriage can be an important phase in one's life course. In traditional China, marriages were arranged by the parents of the two families. It was viewed as an alliance involving the joining of resources, so it was too important to be left to individuals. The young couple had little say in the arranged marriage, and romantic love was not a major concern. If the couple was lucky, love and affection would develop over the course of the marriage. In any event, it was important to bear heirs to the family name and to insure the continuity of the family.

But in the twentieth century, the place of love and romance in marriage has assumed a central position. In this sense, the desires and interests of the couple are now seen as the major determinant of a marriage. A couple may meet in the course of their education or in a place of employment, or through an introduction by others. As a result, in Taiwan and in the United States, marriages are now conducted in a manner familiar to other Americans.

While many Taiwanese marry other Taiwanese, intermarriages are on the rise. In the United States, there are many instances of marriage of those from Taiwan marrying other Chinese. Thus, for example, many Taiwanese have married Cantonese. There are also marriages with Chinese from Hong Kong, Singapore, Southeast Asia, and other areas. In addition, in the United States, many Asian Americans are marrying other Asian Americans who are outside their specific ethnic group. An example might be a Taiwanese American marrying a Japanese American, or a Vietnamese American marrying a Filipino American.

On the other hand, there are also rising numbers of marriage with those who are not Chinese or Asians. Familiarity with others through schools, work, and other encounters provides opportunities for a wider choice in marriage. As a result, in almost every community, there are mixed marriages of those from Taiwan with non-Chinese. In this sense, the Taiwan Chinese mirror the intermarriage that has been occurring with other Chinese Americans and Asian Americans.

With such a development, there are increasing numbers of mixed-race children. In a pluralistic society such as the United States, this is hardly a surprising situation. Many third- or fourth-generation descendants of immigrants are a rich mix of different heritages or ethnicities. This trend means that the parents must negotiate how they will raise the children and the type of religious orientation that the children may assume. It also has led to suggestions that the U.S. Census should henceforth adopt a category for those of mixed parentage. At the present time, one can only check off a single category such as "Asian American," "Hispanic," "American Indian," "African American," and so on. A mixed parentage category would permit people to check off their identity as being exactly that instead of being a single ethnic category. Or, they could check off several categories as a way of indicating their multiple identities. They would then not have to deny any facet of their interracial ancestry.

Within the family, a number of customs are observed with the corresponding rite of passage. That is to say, certain customs may be followed with the different stages in the life of a family. These rites of passage pertain to marriage, birth of a child, the celebration of a birthday, and funerals. Depending upon the family, there may be variations in the observance of these family customs.

The marriage is a good example of the influence of family customs. Marriage is the union of two individuals and two households. When a couple marries, their families are also joined as relatives. For many families, the hope for an auspicious marriage will lead them to check an almanac. Their parents especially, whether in Taiwan or the United States, are likely to consult it and offer advice to the prospective couple. The almanac will describe whether they are a lucky match according to the years of their birth. It functions thus as a horoscope.

For example, the Chinese calendar is based on the lunar year. It has a zodiac of a twelve-year cycle in which there are twelve different animals for each year. These animals are the rat, ox, tiger, rabbit, dragon, snake, horse, sheep, monkey, chicken, dog, and pig. Each animal is then paired with five elements, which are metal, wood, earth, water, and fire. It takes sixty years to complete a full cosmic cycle, which then repeats itself. The Chinese almanac helps to interpret what will be an appropriate day for an event and also offers a suggestion as to whether a marriage will be a lucky one. Individuals born in a year associated with a particular animal will have certain traits that may or may not match with others. Those persons born in the Year of the Rat should marry those born in the Year of the Dragon, Monkey, or the Ox. They should not marry those born in the Year of the Horse. But if a couple really wants to wed, such traditional practices are not likely to deter them.

A wedding is a joyous affair to be celebrated. It signals the start of a family, an important rite of passage in Chinese society. A church wedding or a civil wedding at city hall is followed with a banquet. The guests parade into the restaurant to offer their greetings and wishes for a happy marriage. They may bestow envelopes of money or gifts to the new couple. In the United States, the new couple may have opened a bridal registry with a department store so that they can receive chinaware, linen, appliances, and other needed items without duplication. In the course of the wedding banquet, there may be games and teasing by well-wishers who try to add levity to the event.

In a few cases, if the finances permit and the parents desire it, there may be two wedding banquets—one in the United States and one in Taiwan. This may occur if one or two sets of parents are in Taiwan. One banquet is held for their benefit, while the other is held in the United States for the friends of the couple. During the 1980s, for a while, it was the practice to send the bride off to Taiwan to a cooking class so that she could learn how to prepare traditional Chinese dishes for her new family.

The birth of children is a happy occurrence. Before the birth, the mother is provided with foods that will strengthen her body. There are also food taboos of items that should not be consumed during this time, such as the consumption of lamb. After the birth, foods to restore her strength will be prepared. In this way, the health of mother and child are ensured. The birth of a baby is sure to touch off great excitement, and when the baby is one month old many families celebrate with a first-month party.

YOUTH

For immigrants from Taiwan, a major concern is their children. Their children may be of the 1.5 generation or the second generation. The 1.5 generation is a term borrowed from Korean Americans (*il-chom-o-se*) and refers to those who were born abroad but came to the United States at a young age. The second generation, on the other hand, alludes to those who were born in this country. But regardless of the generation, education is the primary concern of their parents.

Education

Since so many of the Taiwanese parents are professionals, they are fully aware of the importance of an education. In Taiwan, they themselves were the products of academic senior high schools that prepared them to take the national entrance examination for the universities. Fewer than half of those who take the competitive, three-day examination can get into a university or college (Su 1995:7). But even before that examination, they had to take another test when they were at the junior high school level. That standardized school placement examination determined whether they were eligible for academic senior high schools, which could pave the way into the universities. Since the competition was fierce and the number of openings for admission limited, their own experience impressed upon them the necessity to study hard and to learn diligently. They may have had to learn so much information that they felt like "stuffed ducks" (*tianyashi*). Nevertheless, they believe that educational success affects future success in a career. This commitment to education has been transferred to the United States.

Parental Involvement. When Taiwanese parents purchase a home, they seek one in a neighborhood with good schools. Many times the quality of the schools dictates the selection of the area in which they will live. Determination of the quality of schools is gauged by the number of National Merit finalists and semifinalists and their success in obtaining admission to selective universities. This information can be obtained by comparing notes with other Taiwanese parents. Often this means that they will buy a home in a middle-class or upper-class neighborhood. Even though the real estate costs may be very high in that locale, they will simply pick a smaller home so that the children will benefit from the schools in that area.

A very select few who are extremely well-to-do will send their children to the exclusive preparatory or boarding schools in the Northeast. The children might then attend schools such as Phillips (Andover), Phillips Exeter, Deerfield, Groton, and Choate Rosemary, which have a proven track record to Ivy League universities. Other schools would be the Bronx High School of Science, Stuyvesant High School, and Lawrence High School in New York. This result is that, except for during vacation periods and the summers, the children will be separated from their parents who live on the West Coast. But the hope of these parents is that their children can secure early admittance to a very selective university.

During the early preschool years, the parents prefer that relatives such as grandparents or the mother will care for the children. But if the couple is a two-income family with both parents having to work, or no grandparents are located nearby, then they will turn to daycare or childcare centers. The choice of a center is based on its track record as determined from discussion with others. Although some are on the expensive side, if the center teaches skills that will be applicable to elementary schools, the parents will be willing to assume the costs.

Admission of their children to the best college or university possible is the objective of many Taiwanese parents. Educational fairs, lectures, and presentations on college admissions are guaranteed to draw a large and attentive audience. Parents and their children learn to write creative essays on "Why I Want to Attend Harvard" or some other university. As a result, many organizations schedule talks on the topic by college admissions officers. Present at the events are freshmen or upperclassmen who can explain how they got into an Ivy League institution or a selective university such as the Massachusetts Institute of Technology or the California Institute of Technology. Chinese newspapers often carry news stories about the ratings of U.S. universities by magazines such as *U.S. News and World Report.* Or, they may run pieces on student life at a famous university such as Chicago or Princeton.

The parents carefully track the progress of their children to prepare them for the academic courses required for admission to selective colleges and universities. They share information about who are the good teachers from elementary, to intermediate, to high school levels. While all parents emphasize the importance of good grades and academic success, it is often the women who are the most attentive. "Confucian moms" are the Taiwanese equivalent of "education moms" (*kyoiku mama*) in Japan who closely monitor their children's studies. One husband noted that the "Confucian moms are driven: they come home with extra books for their children to read." They recommend books to the children to enrich their knowledge and to supplement what has been learned in school. Some resort to home study books or modules to help their children get an extra edge in their mastery of different academic subjects. Even when the children are watching television, they encourage programs on the educational channels. Computers are purchased to help the children access encyclopedias and become computer literate.

Coaching Schools. In Taiwan, cram schools called *buxiban* are available to help prepare the children to take the competitive national examinations for entry into the public universities. They are modeled on the Japanese cram schools dubbed *juku* in Japanese. The cram schools are essentially private coaching schools to supplement the regular school curriculum. Because the parents are anxious about their children's future, they enroll their sons and daughters in these coaching schools. Every Taiwanese parent knows about them, and they regale their children with tales about how much easier schooling in the United States is in comparison to Taiwan.

But as in Taiwan, coaching schools have appeared in the United States. Modeled on the Japanese and Taiwanese examples, these cram schools now exist in many parts of the country. In fact, cities that have a substantial proportion of Asian immigrants are likely to have them. The Kumon schools throughout the United States are perhaps the best known. Affiliated with the Kumon Educational Institute, the Kumon schools are franchises that operate in many different communities. In the San Francisco Bay area and San Jose area of California alone, in 1995, there were between fifty and seventy-five Kumon schools.

Their format was developed by mathematics teacher Toru Kumon in Japan in the 1950s and introduced into the United States. It emphasizes rapidity and accuracy in test taking. In the mathematics program, students can progress from arithmetic through algebra, trigonometry, and geometry to calculus. The strength of the Kumon schools (*Gongwen shuxue*) is primarily in mathematics, but in recent years, they have also devised a reading comprehension program. The reading program aims to build verbal aptitude and reading ability for materials of increasing complexity and difficulty in vocabulary and expression (*World Journal* 10/5/95:B19).

The format of the programs is relatively simple. Parents and their children receive daily lessons that must be completed. Only when the students demonstrate accuracy and quickness in finishing their problems can they move on to different subject areas at another level. Should they require too much time to complete problem sets or commit too many errors with their lessons, they have not demonstrated mastery of a subject area. They will be given another group of lessons that continues to treat the subject. They will do that set, and even another, all focusing on the same mathematical operations until they show acceptable competence in timing and accuracy. Only then will they be permitted to move on to the next level.

The centers stress that the lessons are to be done daily. The lesson sheets with problems are light and compact. As a result, even when a family goes on a trip, takes a vacation, or is enjoying a holiday, the lessons can be done daily and conveniently. The idea is that a few minutes each day help to cultivate needed skills for the long run. Parents are encouraged to bring their children to the centers to do the lessons and to have them corrected there by the instructors. This can be done after the regular school hours and on Saturdays. That way the students can be weaned away from familiar environments like the home. This also gets them ready to take Scholastic Aptitude Tests (SAT) or American College Testing (ACT) tests in environments similar to the actual examination sites when they are in high school.

These coaching schools are not without their critics. Some observers suggest that the schools are better at teaching rote learning rather than critical, independent thinking and problem solving. In rebuttal, their defenders say that they are merely complementary to the regular school curriculum. The exercises that the students must perform are to reinforce what is taught by their teachers in the regular school day. Moreover, they declare that real life testing situations do reward students for their ability to finish and solve problems accurately. Ultimately, though, the parents of the children are the ones who will decide this issue. And many Taiwanese parents feel these schools do have merit.

In some instances, Taiwanese parents have hired tutors for their children. If several families can band together, they can collectively hire a tutor from the nearby university, college, community college, or high school. The tutor then teaches several children at one of the homes. The tutor can be a professor who is a friend to the parents, but more likely, the tutors are graduate students, exceptional undergraduate students, or substitute teachers. International students, especially those from Taiwan, Hong Kong, Singapore, or China, may be sought as tutors because of their strong skills in mathematics and science. Tutors are also hired to teach English literature, grammar, and creative writing.

If school districts have programs for the advanced or gifted students, the parents will try to steer their children so that they can gain admittance. They welcome the enhanced curriculum and the additional attention on academics in these schools. In recent years, elite universities such as Johns Hopkins and Stanford have developed summer programs for youth who are especially gifted. Testing is used to determine eligibility for these programs. Many Taiwanese parents deem it quite an achievement if their children can secure admission to one of these prestigious programs.

High School Preparation. Once the children are in high school, the parents help them pick out their academic programs. At this level, the emphasis is on courses that are required for college admission to selective universities. This means four years of mathematics, including calculus, if it is offered. Science courses are stressed, such as biology, chemistry, and physics. Also emphasized are literature and social studies classes such as American, English, and world literature; U.S., European, and Asian history; and government. In addition, a foreign language is seen as desirable. It may be French, German, Spanish, or Russian. However, because of the large influx of Asian immigrants and the importance of trade with Asia and the Pacific, some school districts have offered language courses in Mandarin Chinese, Japanese, and Korean.

In general, the children are encouraged to take Advanced Placement (AP) classes that can earn college credits. These may be Advanced Placement courses in biology, chemistry, physics, history, literature, mathematics, and foreign languages. If a nearby university or college offers high school students opportunities to take mathematics or computer science classes, the parents will ask their children to enroll in them. During the summers, some parents enroll their children at courses in summer programs offered by universities such as Johns Hopkins, Harvard, and Stanford. In other words, the taking of coursework that would help when applying to college is always a conscious consideration.

Extracurricular Activities. This heavy focus on academic preparation, however, does not mean that extracurricular activities are neglected. On the contrary, Taiwanese parents know that the very selective and prestigious universities value students who are well rounded. They know that college admissions officers often look for those who can contribute to the richness and diversity of undergraduate student life. As a result, children are often started on a musical instrument at a very young age. The piano and the violin are the most common instruments. Some even are encouraged to learn a second instrument. Parents tell stories of young child prodigies like Sarah Chang and Helen Huang. They point out the artistry of those like Yo-Yo Ma or Midori.

Many music teachers openly admit that Asian parents are among the most dedicated in helping to support music education. The parents see to it that their children enter music competitions and perform at recitals. They buy season tickets for the symphony so that the children can appreciate classical music. Furthermore, they try to get their sons and daughters to try out for positions in a community's junior orchestra or youth symphony. This is very competitive, but the parents apply pressure and encourage their children to try their best. Playing music, they feel, teaches patience and perseverance that can also be applied to academic studies.

In fact, there is a North American Elite Chinese Youth Orchestra that has been organized in the United States by David Wong. Wong, who was born in Taiwan, felt that there was enough talent to create such an orchestra. He selects its young members from auditions in cities such as Los Angeles, San Francisco, New York, and Washington, D.C. With an average age of about sixteen, about half of them are American born and about half are foreign born. Since its formation in 1995, the orchestra has performed in Carnegie Hall and has toured different cities in the United States and Taiwan. Its repertoire includes music from both East and West (D. Lin 1996b:5).

Besides the obligatory music lessons, parents encourage their children to participate in other activities, including forensics with debate or oral inter-pretation, drama or theatric productions, and journalism with the school paper or yearbook. Competition in sports such as tennis and golf are an option. Student government, various cultural and language clubs, and inter-collegiate organizations dealing with the United Nations or the Asian-Pacific region are also possibilities. Volunteer and civic-minded activities in the school and in the community are considered worthwhile, too.

Entering into history day and science fair competitions is also emphasized. Winning recognition in history day competitions that focus on a particular historical theme each year is a way to gain prominence at a school district, county, state, and possibly national level. But even more important than the history day competitions are the science fair competitions. Science is viewed as a basic subject, and to excel in science is is deemed desirable by the parents. Children are often told about the success of others who have won in the extremely competitive and nationally renowned Westinghouse science com-petitions each year.

The greater weight given to science and mathematics is associated with job preferences valued by the parents. Taiwanese parents see jobs with scientific and technical training as affording more security, better income, and greater prestige. They therefore try to direct their children into careers such as medicine, science, engineering, and computer science. Professions in business, law, and education at the university level are also acceptable. While they may let their children take majors in the humanities and the social sciences, they hope that a change in direction will occur later. Or, they think that admission to law school or to business school for an M.B.A. will be a future option.

University Selection. Because success in education is seen as a prerequisite for a success in a career, discussions about the best universities are commonplace. Over and over again, parents talk among themselves about the relative merits of MIT (Massachusetts Institute of Technology) versus Cal Tech (California Institute of Technology), or Harvard versus Yale. Institutional prestige, the number of Nobel Prize winners on its faculty, and the strength of its engineering programs are certain to be debated. The prominence of its medical, business, and law schools also undergo fierce scrutiny. Although admittance to any of the top twenty-five or top fifty, or even select hundred, universities and colleges in the United States is a formidable achievement, the parents prefer to focus on the top ten.

Obviously, not all the children of Taiwanese immigrants can be admitted to an arbitrary ranking of top ten institutions. Many will go to other institutions that are also extremely selective or very selective in their admissions policies. Public universities with lower tuitions can offer a fine undergraduate education as well. The money saved can then be used for graduate school later. As a result, competition to enter the flagship universities in the University of California system is especially fierce. Admission to the University of California at Berkeley or at Los Angeles is among the most cherished hopes of many Taiwanese parents and their children as an alternative to a private university such as Stanford or the California Institute of Technology.

In some ways, this fixation by Taiwanese parents on university education is ironic. Many explain that they feel that the United States is more relaxed and less stressful in its educational system than in Taiwan. The pressure is not as intense as in Taiwan, for the future of high school students to enter public universities does not rest on an extremely competitive university entrance examination. Many options and alternatives are available in the United States. And yet the parents have fashioned anew a pressure cooker of their own for their children.

A Concern with Education. But to the Taiwanese children, the concern about education by their parents is all too obvious. It is the overriding unspoken principle by which their parents operate. A cartoon in the *World*

Journal (*Shijie Ribao*) on August 11, 1996, acknowledged this openly. The cartoon was entitled "A Mother and Child." In one panel, a cheerful mother tells her pleased child, "Dear, mother has bought a lot of playthings for you." In the next panel, the child looks disappointed, for in the gift box, labeled "Made in Taiwan," are playthings entitled *SAT Workbook, Mathematics, Science, Trigonometry, Algebra,* and *English* (*World Journal* 8/11/96:5). In the Taiwanese community, the following observations have been made about "being Taiwanese" or "being Chinese":

"How to be a Perfect Taiwanese Kid (from the first generation perspective)"

1. Score 1600 on the SAT.
2. Play the violin or piano on the level of a concert performer.
3. Apply to and be accepted by 27 colleges.
4. Have three hobbies: studying, studying, and studying.
5. Go to a prestigious Ivy League university and win enough scholarship to pay for it.
6. Love classical music and detest talking on the phone.
7. Become a Westinghouse, Presidential, and eventually a Rhodes Scholar.
8. Aspire to be a brain surgeon.
9. Marry a Taiwanese-American doctor and have perfect, successful children (grandkids for *ahma* and *ahba*!).
10. Love to hear stories about your parents' childhood . . . especially the one about walking 7 miles to school without shoes.

These observations have been widely circulated and always elicit some laughs. But most observers admit that they do capture in a humorous fashion the experience of "growing up Taiwanese." The parents vicariously seem to be positioning their children for entrance to the American equivalent of "*Taida*" or National Taiwan University, one of the most selective universities in Taiwan. Conversely, there is a set of observations about what the children wish their Taiwanese or Chinese parents would be like:

"How to be a Perfect Taiwanese Parent (from the second generation perspective)"

1. Be a little more lenient on the 7 p.m. curfew.
2. Don't ask where the other point went when your child comes home with a 99 course grade on his/her report card.

3. Don't "*ai-yoh*" loudly at your kid's dress habits.

4. Don't blatantly hint about the merits of *Hah-phoo* (Harvard), *Yale-uh* (Yale), *Stan-phoo* (Stanford), and *Emeh-I-Tee* (M.I.T.).

5. Don't reveal all the intimate details of your kid's life to the entire Taiwanese community.

6. Don't ask your child, "What are you going to do with your life?" if he/she majors in a non-science field.

7. Don't give your child a bowl haircut or your daughter two acres of bangs.

8. Don't try to set up your kid on a date in anticipation of their poor taste or inept social skills.

9. Incorporate other phrases besides "Did you study yet?" into your daily conversations with your children.

10. Don't ask all your kid's friends over the age of 21 if they have a boyfriend/girlfriend yet.

The emphasis on academics by Asian parents has attracted the attention of American society. Several years ago, a series of "Doonesbury" cartoons drawn by artist Garry Trudeau drew attention to the scholastic achievements of Asian American students. The other American students viewed them as being mechanical, robotic, and relentless—seeming almost alien and out of this world—in their pursuit of academic success. In one strip, an Asian American student parodied this stereotypic perception of Asians by dryly quipping in a deadpan manner to another student, "Take me to your leader." In another strip, one character, B.D., says that he sees a Vietnamese as just a "geek" like all the other Asians. But a companion corrects him by noting that "not all Asians are Brainiacs" (Trudeau 1996:A9).

Nonetheless, while many Asian Americans have won recognition for their academic attainment, others have not. They are normal, average students as reflected in any student population. For them, however, failure to obtain A's is seen by others as a weakness. And if they do not excel in their classes in science and mathematics, their teachers may be mystified by their less than stellar performance. Many instructors routinely assume that Asian students have no difficulty in quantitative and technical studies. But as with other students, some Asian students have strengths and interests in areas other than the sciences and mathematics.

As the numbers of Asian American students have risen at colleges and universities, their presence has sometimes evoked mixed comments. In the early 1970s, some educators complained that an excessive number of Asians on campuses meant that there would be few majors in the humanities and social sciences. Others referred to MIT as "Made in Taiwan," while UCLA was dubbed the "University of Caucasians Living among Asians." Critics charged that campuses would be cultural deserts if too many Asian students were admitted. They felt that the preoccupation of Asian Americans with the sciences and professional studies resulted in no room for extracurricular activities, leaving universities without any student life.

However, these fears and anxieties have proved to be unfounded. The extracurricular involvement of Asian American high school and college students compares favorably with that of their peers. On campuses throughout the country, Asian American students—many of whom are Taiwanese Americans—have contributed to the enhancement of college life. They perform in school orchestras, drama societies, and debating clubs. They serve in student government, work on student papers and yearbooks, and participate in inner-city tutoring programs. Still others participate in intramural and intercollegiate competition in sports such as fencing, golf, and tennis.

Language

Language is another important concern for immigrants from Taiwan. To be able to converse with someone else in the language they used in Taiwan is to recognize their common roots or origins. It is a way of rekindling a sense of identity or community. And, for some, it is the language that they can use with the greatest ease. But above all, for parents, it is a thread that binds them with their children. As a result, the first-generation immigrants want to see to it that their children can speak the parents' language.

But the second generation does not necessarily reciprocate this parental interest. In many cases, they resent the loss of their free time. This is especially the case as they enter the intermediate or high school grades. At that point, the parents must mobilize arguments to convince the children about the merits of learning a language other than English. First of all, they might say, this is the language that can be used in international trade and other areas. To learn this is to have better chances in securing employment, whether it is for international commerce or to link up with clients from Asia. As a result, it is a very practical skill. Second, it is a way of learning to communicate with grandparents, aunts, uncles, cousins, and other relatives from Taiwan. On visits to see relatives in Taiwan, knowing Chinese, Taiwanese, or Hakka would be helpful.

A third argument that has recently been added is the possibility of earning college credit. Several years ago, the Educational Testing Service in Princeton, New Jersey, announced that it was working on an assessment test for Chinese.

That news received wide currency in the Chinese press, for it indicated that college credit might be earned for learning Chinese well. Today, tests for Chinese and Japanese are available that can earn college credit. But because the examination is for Chinese and not Taiwanese or Hakka, greater emphasis is focused on the study of Mandarin Chinese.

Irrespective of the arguments that parents may use on their children, teaching Chinese is a formidable challenge. Even in households that speak Chinese, the children do not necessarily pick up the language. When they are young, they may freely converse with their parents, relatives, and family friends in Chinese. As they grow older as teenagers, however, they show a reluctance to use the language. Awash in a sea of English, they are embarrassed to use Chinese, which would set them off from their peers. Learning to read and write the characters is especially difficult. One frustrated mother confessed that the best that she and her husband could do was to create an environment for Chinese. If their daughter could learn to listen and to speak Chinese, then she could could be at least "half a Chinese" (Xiao Di 1997: C10).

Teaching children a language can be done in several ways. One method is to have the parents speak it every day at home. By exposing their sons and daughters to a language other than English, they hope that the children can pick up much of the parents' language. If the family can purchase language books through the mail or at a bookstore, that would be helpful as well. Computer-based language programs or videotapes can also be obtained that might help in this process. Moreover, in many communities, cable channels, satellite television, and local television programming permit access to news and entertainment shows from Taiwan that can complement the teaching. Some Chinese newspapers have a children's section with essays by children and others, which can help in language instruction. If one parent, such as a mother, stays at home, language instruction can be handled much more easily.

Another method is to enroll the children in a language school. In the past, most Chinese language schools in the United States taught Cantonese. Mandarin Chinese might be offered for several periods a week because as *guoyu*, it was the national language in Taiwan. But it was only a small part of the curriculum, for Cantonese parents wanted their children to be able to learn mostly Cantonese. Since 1965, as more and more parents from Taiwan and China have arrived in the United States, more schools offer an exclusively Mandarin Chinese language curriculum.

The schools are sponsored by community groups, parents, or churches. The language schools operate daily in the afternoons after the "regular schools" or on weekends. Those that have daily classes can cover more material and can exhibit a greater rigor in their instruction. However, many children do not have time on weekdays due to their regular school studies. The weekend language schools are more popular, for the parents themselves also find it difficult to get away from work to provide the transportation on a daily basis to a Chinese school. The Chinese schools therefore offer their classes for a few hours on Saturday or Sunday. The sites are often borrowed from a school or a church, so a number of classrooms are available. Many churches provide Sunday schools for children, so as long as the Chinese school seeks a different time, they have ample classroom space for instruction. Moreover, both the schools and churches have adequate parking for the parents and the children.

Curriculum. The Chinese schools obtain most of their books and teaching materials from Taiwan. The Republic of China has an interest in helping overseas Chinese maintain their facility with the Chinese language. They also want to help foreign-born Chinese learn the language of their parents. The Overseas Chinese Office and branches of the Taibei Economic and Cultural Representative Office in the United States help subsidize some of the schools in their operations and in their acquisition of curriculum materials. On occasion, Taibei provides opportunities for instructors and administrators in the Chinese schools to visit Taiwan and become acquainted with innovative teaching methods.

Not all the teaching materials come from Taiwan. A few schools purchase their books from Hong Kong, China, and Singapore. Some even develop complementary materials for their own students. But because the number of students is small, the cost of developing the materials and publishing them is high. In general, it is easier to subscribe to a sequence of materials that has already been developed and tested. And books published in Taiwan are easily available.

In 1976, a Southern California Council of Chinese Schools was created to acquire textbooks from Taiwan and to develop supplementary materials. It also organizes workshops for teachers and plans summer camps. In 1992, there were ninety-four Chinese language schools in Southern California alone. The Southern California Council that was created in 1976 now has links to more than eighty Chinese schools and more than a thousand teachers. There are more than twenty thousand students, most of whom are of the elementary school age. The area affiliated with the council has even extended to Phoenix, Arizona (C. Huang 1994:385–86).

Because most of the books originate from Taiwan, the students are exposed to a great deal of information about China. Its history and traditions are outlined in the lessons. Social studies subjects such as Chinese geography, society, and customs are explored. Chinese philosophy and its religions are explained. Stories about Chinese heroes, folklore, and mythical legends are included to capture the interest of the students. In all the books, moral and civic values concerning the importance of family, obedience to parents, respect for authority, and regard for education are stressed. These are Confucian values, and the life and teachings of Confucius receive extended treatment. Many schools observe Confucius's Birthday and Teacher's Day, which is commemorated in Taiwan on September 28. The day honors Confucius as a preeminent teacher and all who follow in his footsteps as teachers.

Language instruction, however, is the raison d'etre for the Chinese schools. The cultural information in the books is seen as a means to an end, which is the learning of Chinese. Although some might say that the exposure to Chinese values can be just as important as, if not more important than, the learning of the Chinese language, many parents do not see it that way. As a result, the focus is on the spoken and written aspects of the language. This emphasis nonetheless is the cause of much discussion and deliberation in many of the language schools. Teachers, parents, students, and community members may all be drawn in.

One difficult issue involves how the pronunciation of Chinese words is to be taught. There are several methods. One is the *Guoyu zhuyin fuhao* or National Phonetic Symbols system. This method employs symbols drawn from Chinese characters to represent the sounds for a word. By combining "initials" and "finals," students can learn how a word is to be pronounced. This system favors those who have a good knowledge of Chinese characters. It is the method favored on Taiwan and is still used there today. Some Chinese language newspapers, such as the *World Journal* (*Shijie Ribao*), have the *Guoyu zhuyin fuhao* symbols placed next to Chinese characters in their children's section to help children learn the Mandarin Chinese pronunciation.

Another method is the Wade-Giles system of romanization. Romanization refers to the use of the alphabet. Devised in the nineteenth century by Thomas Wade and Herbert Giles, it was the approach most commonly used in Great Britain and the United States to represent the pronunciation of Chinese words. The catalogue cards in most libraries in this country, including that of the Library of Congress, used to employ this approach. However, many students familiar with English are confused by its rendering of the *b* sound as *p*, while the *p* sound is represented as *p'* with an apostrophe. A *k* and *t* without apostrophes denote the *g* and *d* sounds, while *k'* and *t'* with apostrophes denote the *k* and *t* sounds.

After the United States and China established formal diplomatic relations, most universities and colleges adopted the *Hanyu pinyin* or Chinese Phonetic Alphabet system of romanization to teach the pronunciation for Chinese words. Also using the alphabet that is familiar to American students, *pinyin* has an advantage over the Wade-Giles system. Without resorting to the use of apostrophes, *p*, *k*, and *t* represent the *p*, *k*, and *t* sounds. And *b*, *k*, and *d* represent the *b*, *k*, and *d* sounds. This system of romanization is less confusing to students familiar with English. Yale University had developed a Yale romanization system very similar to China's *Hanyu pinyin* system, but its use was largely restricted to a series of language textbooks.

Today most scholars, publishers, and journals have adopted China's *Hanyu pinyin* system as the preferred method of romanization. The *New York Times*, other newspapers, news agencies, and the media have also elected to use China's romanization system. Under this system, China's former leader Teng Hsiao-p'ing is spelled as Deng Xiaoping while China's capital Peking is spelled as Beijing. China's first empire, the Ch'in dynasty from 221–206 B.C., is represented as the Qin dynasty (DeFrancis 1990; Bryant 1992).

With so many systems of romanization, which one should Chinese language schools use? Because many of the teachers in the schools were themselves educated in Taiwan, they are familiar with the *Guoyu zhuyin fuhao* symbols system. As a result, they prefer to use this method to teach the pronunciation of Chinese words and characters. This is not a romanized system, however. And conveniently, the textbooks from Taiwan provide the symbols in miniature alongside the Chinese characters to help students pronounce the words. However, for students reared in the United States, these symbols look just as enigmatic as the Chinese words that they are trying to learn. So many of them write their own English pronunciations right next to the Chinese characters and ignore Taiwan's *Guoyu zhuyin fuhao* symbols.

Taiwan's *Guoyu zhuyin fuhao* system does have a romanized counterpart. It is the National Romanized Phonetic Alphabet or the *Guoyu luomazi* system. While it contains some features similar to the Wade-Giles and Yale romanization systems, its spelling scheme is considered very complicated. That being the case, it has not been widely used outside of Taiwan. Even in Taiwan, it has only received limited use as a teaching tool for foreign students, as the major emphasis even for them is on the *Guoyu zhuyin fuhao* system. The American Overseas Chinese Elementary School Textbooks (*Meizhou huaqiao xiaoxue jiaokeshu*) series of Mandarin Chinese readers (*Guoyu*), used in some language schools in the United States, has the *Guoyu zhuyin fuhao* symbols next to the Chinese characters. But students can refer to the back of each reader where the English romanization from the *Guoyu luomazi* system is listed next to the *Guoyu zhuyin fuhao* symbols.

The teachers in the Chinese language schools generally do not use any of the romanization systems. They are not trained teachers or professional linguists. Most of them have other employment or are housewives. Because they are interested in teaching Chinese to the younger generation, they are willing to assume duties in the classroom. What they lack in training, they make up in enthusiasm and dedication. There can be little doubt that they are eager to help the youth. They fall back upon their own experiences as first-generation immigrants and tout the *Guoyu zhuyin fuhao* system to the dismay of their students. If the students do not know the system well, it must be reviewed with them each fall. The different romanization systems are for the most part not used at all.

The question of whether Taiwan's *Guoyu zhuyin fuhao* should be replaced by a romanization system has stimulated a great deal of discussion in the Chinese language newspapers. One recent article, for example, mentioned that the nonromanized *Guoyu zhuyin fuhao* was easy to use for those who already knew Chinese characters. But for overseas Chinese and those in other countries, a romanization system such as China's *Hanyu pinyin* was easier to use. Having the use of the alphabet to aid in pronouncing Chinese characters and words actually helped to promote international use of Chinese (Z. Huang 1996:S3). Interestingly, in recent years, some educators on Taiwan have advocated wider use of romanization by students there as a way of helping them to strengthen their knowledge of English.

When Chinese language schools are located close to colleges and universities, undergraduate or graduate students from Taiwan are recruited as teachers. The foreign students receive a modest compensation that can help with their tuition and living expenses. Or the small salaries can provide a little additional spending money. The students from Taiwan bring new people and fresh ideas to the school. Being somewhat younger, they are closer to the age of the youth that they are teaching. The parents hope that they can help to bridge the generation gap, for they know more about contemporary movies, songs, and popular fashion. Furthermore, they may have skills in performing folk dances, playing Chinese musical instruments, or teaching martial arts.

Another difficult issue to be resolved is the kind of Chinese characters to be used. Taiwan uses the standard style or *kaishu* characters, which had been used in China since the Han dynasty. It is still widely used in Hong Kong, Macau, and among communities of Chinese outside of China, including those in the United States. But in China simplified style or *jianzi* characters have been used, especially after 1956. In this style, fewer strokes are used for the characters. The idea is that simplified style characters utilizing fewer strokes are easier to learn than the traditional standard style characters. That would therefore promote greater literacy among China's people. The simplified style characters are used today in both China and Singapore.

In American colleges and universities, students of Chinese are generally taught both styles. Some teachers prefer to teach the standard style, feeling that it allows students to read the traditional characters that have been used for most of Chinese history. The students can also read the materials published in Taiwan, Hong Kong, and the Chinese community in the United States. On the other hand, some teachers like the simplified style because it is easier to master. They feel it is a convenient strategy to prepare the students for eventually learning the traditional, standard style characters. Students can be exposed to newspapers or publications from China and feel that they can read the characters that more than a billion Chinese are reading. Regardless of the style that is initially taught, students of Chinese in universities are eventually exposed to both styles of characters.

For the Chinese language schools, teachers and parents prefer to use the traditional, standard style characters that are used in Taiwan. First of all, the language books to which they have convenient access are published in that format. Second, the Chinese language papers in the United States all use that style of characters. If they subscribe to newspapers and magazines from Taiwan or Hong Kong, they will also be printed in that mode. Finally, the teachers and parents feel that standard style characters afford continuity with the past. The philosophy, history, poetry, and literature in Chinese civilization can be most readily accessed through the standard style characters.

School Activities. The language schools in some ways exist as much for the parents as for the children. While language instruction is the overriding theme, the schools provide many other activities. Curriculum units on calligraphy, folk dancing, Chinese music, Chinese painting, and the martial arts are taught. Community people with these skills or students from Taiwan are encouraged to participate in the school and share their knowledge with the youth. To the extent that the children can learn these skills, the schools become a community resource. During the Chinese New Year, the Mid-Autumn Festival, and on other special occasions, the schools can help to provide entertainment at the cultural programs.

Various measures are used to encourage the students to be diligent in their studies. Assemblies or meetings are held where prizes may be awarded to the top students in each classroom. In some instances, if the resources are available, all the students will receive a small gift. It may be a Chinese character dictionary, a notebook, some cards or bookmarkers, and so on. If the budget permits, light refreshments and snacks are offered to the students every week; otherwise, it might be on special occasions. Chinese festivals and holidays, including Confucius's Birthday, are causes for celebration, and the schools will observe them so that the students can learn about the rich Chinese cultural heritage.

Parents can also participate in activities at the school sites. While they are waiting for their children to finish their lessons, they and other community members can learn about Chinese martial arts such as *qigong,* a type of deep breathing exercises, and *taijiquan,* a graceful form of exercise. Others might take a course on calligraphy, Chinese painting, or Chinese cooking. Parents who have no interest in those activities can help with the preparation of refreshments for the students at recess or at the end of the school day. Some will just socialize with other parents and community members and pass the time away. Occasional fundraisers may be held to make some money to help the school. At one Chinese language school fundraiser that featured various foods such as baked goods, Taiwanese dishes, and dim sum (*dianxin*) pastries, the organizers promised that "what they should have, they will have (*yingyou jinyou*)."

If the schools have enough students and support, they will have cultural programs and fundraisers. The cultural programs are a way of demonstrating that the students have learned something about their cultural heritage. It validates the idea that the schools have successfully fulfilled their function of inculcating a sense of identity to the students that can now be shared with the community. The fundraisers are a means to raise funds for the schools' operations. But beyond whether a lot of money is raised or not, they are a way to get the parents and supporters together in a cooperative effort. The solidarity and common sense of purpose that is developed can be beneficial for the schools.

Study Tours. Sending the children to Taiwan during the summer is another way of teaching them Chinese rather than tutoring them at home or sending to them to Chinese school. While parents may choose to send their children to stay with relatives or friends, there is another way. The Republic of China sponsors a summer program for overseas Chinese youth to travel there and learn a little about Chinese language, history, and culture. It is formally called the Language Training and Study Tour.

The students, from ages eleven to twenty-three, can learn Mandarin Chinese at beginning, intermediate, and advanced levels. They will also be exposed to Chinese calligraphy, painting, art, music, dance, drama, martial arts, and food. There are also games, sports, competitions, tours, visits to scenic sights, and other activities. For part of the time, the students are housed at the Jiantan Overseas Youth Activities Center. Then, they are taken for a tour of the famous and historic sites around the island.

The program is very popular. More parents want to send their children to Taiwan than the program can accept. This is despite the costs that in 1997 ranged from $1,150 to $1,350, depending on the age category (*World Journal* 2/24/97:B8). While the program fosters an appreciation for Chinese language and culture, that is only part of the reason why parents are so enthusiastic about this opportunity for summer study. The other reason is that they want their children to form friendships with other Chinese in the program. If the youth are of college age, the parents hope that romantic matches with other Chinese might occur. As a result, some wags have dubbed this program the "Loveboat Tour." Nonetheless, the success of this program has even led China to try to initiate a similar program for overseas Chinese.

College Courses. Still another way to learn Chinese is to have the youth learn it when they enter a college or university. Because of widespread interest in Asia and the Pacific as a region for business and investment, many universities have expanded offerings in Asian languages such as Japanese, Chinese, and Korean. At the university level, a comprehensive language program offers many courses on speaking and reading Chinese in its modern and classical prose styles. Students can read modern literature or prose, poetry, and historical documents for different periods.

Because the college instruction is more rigorous and systematic, students learn quickly. They must master more characters at a faster pace because the teachers are more demanding. If they desire good grades, they must spend time memorizing the characters and idiomatic expressions. Basic vocabularies must be learned so that students can both speak and read. Language laboratories and audiotapes help reinforce the learning. In most cases, romanization is used and it is usually the *Hanyu pinyin* system. For all these reasons, two years of Chinese instruction at the university level is easily the equivalent of six to nine years at community-operated Chinese language schools.

If college students can spend at least one summer or one year abroad learning Chinese, their language skills and comprehension will be significantly advanced. Many universities suggest one to two years of study in the United States before going abroad to Taiwan or China for further study. There are many U.S. programs for studying Chinese in Taiwan, one of the most famous and successful being the Inter-University Program for Chinese Language Studies in Taibei administered by Stanford University. It is a university consortium with participating members such as Harvard, Columbia, and the University of Chicago. Many parents have marveled at how fluent the youth have become in Chinese after only a summer or year abroad in Taiwan.

Taiwanese American parents invest heavily in their children's education and want their children to learn the Chinese language or Mandarin. The rewards can be high, for the children are on a track to a fine university and hopefully to an outstanding career. At the same time, these parental desires place a heavy burden on the children and may have psychological costs. Some Taiwanese youth claim that there is a lack of communication with their parents. They complain that opportunities for self-expression and social development are restricted. Their immigrant parents are living their American life vicariously through their children. In rebellion, there have been middle-class Taiwanese youth who have joined juvenile gangs in Southern California. In many ways the tension and negotiation between Taiwanese parents and youth are characteristic of other immigrant populations. The tremendous emphasis on education has both its benefits and its costs. But on the whole, few Taiwanese American parents would wish to change their emphases.

3

Living in America

Aside from the family, various networks through associations, the media, and temples or churches are important in expediting the adjustment and adaptation of the Taiwan immigrants to the United States. The common term for network is *guanxi*, which refers to relationships or bonds. One might say it is akin to "connections." The *guanxi* among immigrants from Taiwan may be based on being in the same class at a certain high school, or in the same graduating class at a university before their migration to the United States. There are also festivals that play a key role in linking the lives of Taiwanese Americans.

ASSOCIATIONS

Associations are voluntary organizations that can be helpful in the adaptation of immigrants to another society. Some references to native place migrant associations employ the German phrase *landsmannschaften* for this occurrence. In the nineteenth and twentieth centuries, associations were especially helpful to Cantonese immigrants who had arrived in the United States. Since many had entered as single men, without the support of a family or a network of relatives, associations provided a useful substitute.

Associations were organized according to many different principles—often on the basis of region or district, ethnicity, surname, or occupation. Thus, there were associations for those from the Four Districts (Siyi) or Zhongshan areas of Guangdong. The Hakka, who traditionally in Guangdong had been distinct from the *bendi* or local residents, maintained their own associations.

In addition, there were associations for those who might have a common family last name, such as Zhang or Zheng (Chang), Huang or Wang (Wong), Mei (Moy), Wu (Ong), or Li (Lee). Finally, associations were also formed for those who were employed as restaurant owners, laundry workers, or businessmen.

But the immigrants from Taiwan are somewhat different. Arriving in the period since the 1960s, many came with their spouses and families and were therefore not as dependent upon the traditional associations that had been established by the Cantonese. Moreover, they were not restricted to bachelor status as had been the case before World War II because of exclusionary policies or antimiscegenation laws. Furthermore, with their high degree of education, professional training, and middle-class status, they did not need to affiliate with immigrants from Taiwan, China, Hong Kong, or the older Cantonese community. Many are much more acquainted with the West and many have a command of the English language.

In fact, it could be noted that the immigrants from Taiwan might find the traditional Cantonese organizations difficult to get used to. They do not speak the dialect, and their backgrounds are different. It could also be said that they have a different version of Chinese culture in the way that people from Hong Kong and various parts of China have different versions of Chinese culture. Also, coming from a different period in time, they do not have as great a need for the locality-type associations that were so important until recently.

This is not to say that there are no immigrants from Taiwan in the traditional complex of Cantonese associations. In fact, some join to broaden their network of acquaintances. Others seek the members in these organizations as prospects for potential clients in insurance, stocks, or financial planning. Nor is it to say that the arrivals from Taiwan do not form associations. They do have their own associations, but they are not as dependent upon them as the older Cantonese. They turn to their associations for social friendship, networking opportunities, and the chance to affiliate with people who speak the same dialect and are familiar with the same Taiwan experience. In this sense, associations based on common interests can help them maintain a sense of identity.

Regional and Dialect Associations

For the early Chinese community, regional and dialect associations were important organizations. Their members could turn to people from the same area for help and sustenance. When occasions required a communal response, the associations could be mobilized quickly. For the Taiwanese immigrants, the closest parallel to these regional associations are various Taiwanese associations. An example is the Taiwanese Association of America (*Meiguo Taiwan Tongxianghui*). Started in 1971, it had sixty-six local branches under six regional councils in 1996. With its headquarters in Marietta, Georgia, its purpose is to promote the fellowship and welfare of the Taiwanese community. It also hopes to nurture an interest in the history, language, and culture of Taiwan in America.

With chapters scattered throughout the country, the individual chapter's activities may vary according to its geographical location and its membership. These may include seminars, talks, social events, and forums on matters of local concern. The national organization sets up summer conferences and an annual meeting each year. The local chapters try to cooperate with other Taiwanese organizations to develop common policies on issues of mutual interest. The Taiwanese Association of America publishes a *TAA Bulletin* in English and Mandarin between six and twelve times a year. In 1996, it claimed that this bulletin was mailed to about seven thousand members. Local chapters may also issue their own newsletters.

An example of a social event might be the Chinese New Year's Party held by the Taiwanese Association in Seattle, Washington, on February 27, 1996. Held at a high school in Mercer Island, the party featured a television personality from Southern California and several choir and community groups on its program. Among the participants for the event were a Taiwanese language school, a Taiwanese religious group, the Taiwanese Women's Association, and the University of Washington Taiwanese Student Association. The festivities included singing, a play, dancing, a raffle drawing, and a dinner (*World Journal* 1/13/96:27). Another example might be the Taiwanese Association of Northern California for the Southeastern San Francisco Bay area. In May 1996, they celebrated Mother's Day at a seafood restaurant in San Leandro, California. The program included singing and other performances (*World Journal* 5/8/96:B6).

In recent years, some of the Taiwanese associations have been raising funds to open Taiwanese cultural centers. The Taiwanese Association of Houston raised $300,000 in 1993 and established a Taiwanese Community Center (*Taiwanren Huodong Zhongxin*). In the San Francisco Bay area, Fresno, California, and other locales, there are similar efforts. But the earliest attempt in this direction was launched by the Taiwanese Association of Greater New York City in 1986. It founded a Taiwan Center in Flushing, New York, to promote a sense of Taiwanese identity. This was done by providing information about current affairs in Taiwan. However, the facility ran into financial problems in the 1990s. The Taiwan government then stepped in to help secure a loan to save it (Lai 1996:50).

Another regional-type organization is the Taiwan Benevolent Association of America (*Quanmei Taiwan Tongxiang Lianyihui*). Founded in 1978, this organization is open to those who came from or lived in Taiwan. Unlike the Taiwanese associations that became more critical of the ruling Nationalist government in Taiwan from the 1970s to the 1990s, this organization is supportive of the government. In 1989, it had twelve chapters and twenty thousand members. Each year, the organization holds an annual meeting at one of the different chapters. Noted speakers from Taiwan and elsewhere participate in these gatherings (Lai 1996:53). Local chapters may provide assistance for newcomers from Taiwan, sponsor social events and talks, and organize summer camps and sports activities.

Complementing the Taiwanese associations, there is a North American Taiwanese Women's Association (NATWA), which started in 1988 with headquarters in Berwyn, Pennsylvania, and now has chapters throughout the United States and Canada. It seeks to promote gender equality and to advance the status of Taiwanese American women. To this end, it encourages participation in the public arena. It holds an annual national convention and issues a *NATWA Newsletter* in Chinese several times a year. From August 18 to 21, 1996, it held its eighth annual meeting in San Francisco. Three important themes that were treated were emotional intelligence, the women's conference in Beijing, and the sharing of responsibility and strength of women. Events included wine tasting, special theme evenings, dancing, golf, and karaoke singing. There were also opportunities for trips to San Francisco, the redwood forests, and the Napa vineyards (Li and Lin 1996:7).

Finally, there are the Hakka organizations. The Hakka are a people from Guangdong who have migrated to Taiwan and maintained a separate identity through the years. In the past, the Hakka in the United States have maintained separate organizations apart from the Cantonese from Guangdong. The Hakka from Taiwan now in the United States are no different. There are several of these Hakka organizations, including the Taiwanese Hakka Friendship Association of America (*Quanmei Taiwan Kejia Lianyihui*) formed in 1984 and the Hakka Fellow Townsmen's Association of America (*Quanmei Kejia Tongxianghui*) formed in 1988. There is also a Taiwanese Hakka Association or *Taiwan Kejia Hui* for Southern California (Lai 1996: 51–52). In 1991, a Taiwan Hakka Association for Public Affairs in North America was formed. Its purpose is to further the interests of the Hakka through political and cultural activities. It hopes to help preserve the

Hakka language and culture and sends out a newsletter in Chinese several times a year.

Alumni Associations

Education is very highly valued in Taiwan. A good career and a successful life are seen as predicated upon entry to a good university or college. From early childhood, parents are concerned that their children will do well enough on the national examinations to gain entrance to college. Parents will go to Confucian or Buddhist temples to ask for success in their children's academic performance. They might even go to an oracle or soothsayer to ask them to ascertain how their children will do.

The entrance examination for colleges and universities is offered once a year to all the senior high school graduates. High marks determine entry into prestigious universities and selective departments. Some of the most sought after public universities in Taiwan are National Taiwan University (*Taiwan Daxue*) and National Tsing Hua University (*Qinghua Daxue*). There are also good private universities such as Fu-jen Catholic University (*Furen Daxue*) and Tunghai University (*Donghai Daxue*).

In the United States, there are many alumni of these universities. Others have graduated from such public and private institutions as National Chengchih University (*Zhengzhi Daxue*), National Taiwan Normal University (*Shifan Daxue*), National Cheng Kung University (*Chenggong Daxue*), Soochow University (*Dongwu Daxue*), Tamkang University (*Danjiang Daxue*), and the Chinese Culture University (*Zhongguo Wenhua Daxue*). In California, there even exists a Federation of Alumni of Chinese Universities and Institutes (*Zhongguo Dazhuan Xiaoyou Lianhehui*) which is a federation of the different alumni associations (Lai 1996:55).

But regardless of which college or university it may be, the alumni are well organized here in the United States. They hold many events for the alumni, such as annual meetings with symposia, speeches, dinners, and entertainment. Attendance at these events provides opportunities to learn about classmates and to gain new information. It may even lead to the possibilities for new employment or attractive business opportunities. The alumni who attend these functions may drive across a state or even fly across the country to participate in the events, which have been carefully publicized to ensure a large crowd.

An alumni meeting for National Cheng Kung University in May of 1997 may have been a good example. Sponsored by the Northern California

Alumni Association for the university, the event was held in a hotel. Not only were prominent alumni present, but officials from the Taibei Economic and Cultural Office and the Nationalist Party also attended. Besides reminiscing about past experiences, the alumni took pride in the scholarships that were awarded. The evening's program was festive with prize drawings and karaoke singing as well (Dai and Bai 1997:B3).

However, it is not just the college or university alumni who meet. In some cases, the alumni from some of the high schools, such as the Taibei First Girls' High School, also are organized and hold annual events. Like their college counterparts, they may hold receptions at a fancy hotel, banquets, addresses, and other activities. The school banner may be prominently displayed. Those who attend have the chance to meet their former classmates' families and get caught up on news in other communities or developments in Taiwan. They can also reminisce about school experiences in Taiwan.

Illinois provides a case example of the importance of alumni organizations. It has alumni associations for the Taibei First Girls' High School, National Taiwan University, National Tsinghua University, National Chiao Tung University (*Jiaotung Daxue*), Soochow University, and National Cheng Kung University. There are also chapters for the alumni of National Cheng Chi University, National Chung Hsing University (*Zhongxing Daxue*), National Taiwan Normal University, Tunghai University, Feng-chia University (*Fengjia Daxue*), and Chung Yuan Christian University (*Zhongyuan Daxue*). In addition there are alumni associations for doctors and health professionals from the National Taiwan University Medical College and the National Defense Medical Center (Chinese American Librarians Association 1995:36–39). In short, many of the key universities and colleges in Taiwan are represented in Illinois, and this list of alumni associations is hardly exhaustive for other regions in the United States.

Overall, alumni associations are important networks for Taiwan immigrants in the United States. They help in securing jobs and open the pathways for social activities and other possibilities. As a result, there are frequent reunions, meetings, and social events. Prominent guest speakers may appear, scheduled along with nice meals, social dancing, symposia, and other happenings. Particularly noteworthy graduates who have achieved great success may be recognized and honored. The schools and universities in Taiwan may also use this occasion to raise funds or to ask for donations and support from their alumni in the United States. Their representatives at the same time give reports on happenings back in Taiwan.

Student Organizations

In the earliest phase of migration from Taiwan, students formed a substantial group. On many university campuses, there already existed Chinese clubs for the American-born Chinese. But as the numbers of students from Hong Kong, Taiwan, Southeast Asia, and China increased, interesting changes occurred. In fact, the history of Chinese student organizations in U.S. colleges and universities mirrors the shifting composition of the Chinese community in America.

In the early stage of the 1950s and 1960s, campuses usually had two Chinese student organizations, one for the American-born Chinese—often called the ABC's—and one for the foreign-born Chinese. The latter were sometimes referred to as the FOB's for "fresh-off the boat." Today that is no longer true, as they should properly be labeled FOP's for "fresh-off the plane." The organization for the American-born students might be called the Chinese Students Club, while that for the foreign-born Chinese students—often from Taiwan and Hong Kong—was simply called the Chinese Overseas Students Association.

But there are now many other Chinese student clubs. While the Chinese student clubs for the American-born Chinese continue to exist, the foreign-born students' clubs have changed considerably. They were forced to confront the changes in the background of the Chinese students. For example, in one case, the Chinese Overseas Students Association (COSA) alternated the presidency each semester. For one semester, the post would go to a student from Hong Kong. During the next semester, the post would rotate to a student from Taiwan. This complicated arrangement continued for a number of years. While it resulted in a larger Chinese Overseas Students Association with a greater membership and treasury, it also meant that the presidents and officers barely had enough time to learn how to administer the club before their terms were over.

There were also occasional conflicts and frictions. Many times these occurred because of differences in language, political status, and cultural background. Thus, at the Chinese Overseas Students Association meetings, a vexing issue was whether Cantonese or Mandarin should be spoken as the language for club meetings. Hong Kong students preferred Cantonese, but students from Taiwan sometimes argued that Mandarin was *guoyu*, the "national language." As a compromise, English might be used, but that was not deemed satisfactory either. Only the American-born Chinese who had joined COSA felt comfortable with the use of English.

The differences in political status were also important. Students from Taiwan celebrated "Double Ten." This phrase, called *shuangshi jie*, refers to October 10, 1911. October is the tenth month, and it is the tenth day, hence "Double Ten." On this date there was the outbreak of a revolution that triggered the overthrow of the Qing dynasty and the establishment of the Chinese republic. Unfortunately, this republican era would be troubled by warlordism and later civil war. Nonetheless, the Republic of China on Taiwan sees "Double Ten" as the equivalent of independence day from the alien Manchus who had ruled over them since 1644. As a result, Chinese calendars in Taiwan are dated from 1911 as the pivotal year. Thus, 1997 is referred to as *zhonghua minguo bashiliu nian* or "the eighty-sixth year of the Republic of China." But students in the United States who came from the British colony of Hong Kong did not see why they needed to celebrate this day.

Finally, there is the matter of differences in cultural background. Students from Hong Kong have a greater acquaintance with the English language and Western influences. Hong Kong is a free port with unbridled capitalism, and its residents are exposed to a wide array of multinational corporations and tourists from Europe, North America, and Australia. Students from Taiwan, on the other hand, come from a background that has comparatively less exposure to the West. As a result, in communication on an interpersonal level and in the scheduling of movies and cultural programs, there are always compromises that must be negotiated. Should the movies that are shown be in Cantonese or Mandarin Chinese? Even if the cultural programs are a mix of Cantonese and Taiwanese performances, which language should the emcees or masters of ceremonies use for the audience? Should it be bilingual in Mandarin Chinese and Cantonese, or trilingual with English added in?

In the 1970s, college and university campuses witnessed a greater influx of Chinese students from Southeast Asia. The Chinese Overseas Students Association that we discussed tried to incorporate these students from Southeast Asia by changing its administrative structure. While still having elected presidents from Taiwan and Hong Kong on alternating semesters, it established vice-president positions for the contingents from Hong Kong, Taiwan, Singapore, Malaysia, and Indonesia. But when the number of students from China increased, and some students from Taiwan favored a distinctive Taiwanese perspective in the 1980s, the structure collapsed. Today, there are separate clubs for the Chinese students from Hong Kong, Singapore, Taiwan, and China. The students from Indonesia belong to a separate club, and they can join with those from Malaysia in Asian Bible or Buddhist study groups as well.

There are now many Taiwanese student associations at colleges and universities. On the West Coast, for example, there are Taiwanese student organizations at the University of California, Berkeley, the California Institute of Technology, and Stanford University. In the Midwest, there is representation at institutions such as the University of Chicago, Northwestern University, and the University of Missouri. On the East Coast, the Ivy League universities such as Harvard, Yale, Brown, Pennsylvania, and Cornell all have such organizations. So do MIT, the State University of New York at Buffalo, and the University of Maryland. In the South, Duke University, Texas A & M University, the University of Texas, and Louisiana State University also have such organizations, indicating the spread of students and immigrants from Taiwan throughout the United States.

The activities of these Taiwanese student organizations are quite varied. While they include students from Taiwan, they also include Taiwanese Americans who are interested in their own identity. An example of this is the Yale Taiwanese Club. Founded in 1991, it is officially known as the Yale College Taiwanese Club, and its members are interested in Taiwan's history and culture. The club offers language instruction, explores Taiwanese American and Asian American issues, and features occasional speakers. For recreation, its members watch movies, make trips to New York's Chinatown or "Little Taibei," and hold dumpling dinners or tea and dessert socials. They even offer Taiwanese Club T-shirts for those who desire them (Yale Taiwanese Students Association 1997).

These activities are very similar to those of the Northwestern Taiwanese American Students Club. That organization offers students an opportunity to learn about current affairs and the history and culture of Taiwan. Its members participate in Asian American Heritage Month and show movies such as director Ang Lee's *Eat Drink Man Woman*. In addition, they have doughnut sales, intramural softball, and other social activities (Northwestern Taiwanese Students Association 1997). The Harvard-Radcliffe Taiwanese Cultural Society, on the other hand, holds volleyball tournaments, cultural workshops, and special lectures. Social activities are important, and there are food fests, dumpling get-togethers, and senior picnics (Harvard Taiwanese Students Association 1997).

Many of the Taiwanese student clubs have activities with other Taiwanese clubs in the same state or region. They exchange information, have opportunities to meet, and enjoy the networking and social interaction. A Taiwan Students' Association of America or *Quanmei Taiwan Tongxuehui* was formed in 1985 (Lai 1996:52). An Intercollegiate Taiwanese American Students Association (ITASA) was also established with the same goal in 1991. While it was started originally to explore Taiwanese culture and language, it has moved into other directions as well. Besides offering speakers and forums on various topics, the group organizes dances, dinners, and trips. In the past few years, annual conferences have been held on different campuses such as Brown University to permit students from throughout the country to mingle and meet.

Professional and Business Organizations

Aside from the alumni associations, there exist many professional organizations for those from Taiwan. Since so many of these alumni are employed in middle-class occupations such as education, engineering, financial management, business, and so on, their organizations reflect these vocations. Nationwide in the United States, there is a great profusion of professional organizations that have been created for immigrants from Taiwan. Depending on locale, however, the number of these organizations may vary. In California, New York, New Jersey, and Texas there is an abundance of them. In other communities, there may not be as many. In these cases, the Taiwanese may join organizations with other Chinese from Hong Kong, China, and Southeast Asia.

In general, these professional and business organizations have several functions. First, they can facilitate the exchange of professional or specialized information among the members. This keeps members current in terms of knowledge and expertise. It may also help competitiveness for those who are in business. Newsletters and bulletins complement the meetings, and forums help to spread information. A second function is to protect the interests of their members. By banding together collectively, they can address policies or practices that can affect them negatively. They can lobby or apply pressure on agencies, politicians, or individuals to try to negotiate a compromise or effect a better result. Finally, they provide an opportunity for their members to meet and socialize with others who may have a common background. The events that they organize are always partly for professional and partly for social purposes. Overall, though, the professional and business organizations can help Taiwanese immigrants in their adaptation and adjustment to the United States.

Many of the immigrants from Taiwan were originally students, who later secured teaching positions at American universities. As a result, these faculty members later took a lead in creating Taiwanese faculty or educational organizations on different campuses. Some might be informal groups, while others are much more formally organized. In 1980, the North American Taiwanese Professors' Association (NATPA) or *Bei Meizhou Taiwanren Jiaoshou Xiehui* was founded to promote the dissemination of scientific and professional knowledge and to encourage educational exchanges. It also fosters contact with scholars in Taiwan and emphasizes research on Taiwan. At a meeting in August 1996, for example, it had as its speakers the president of the Academica Sinica, a prestigious honorary society in Taiwan, and several legislators from Taiwan. The organization also aims to further the general welfare of the Taiwanese in both the United States and Taiwan.

Different states and areas have their own chapters. The Chicago chapter, for example, claimed a membership of five hundred in 1995 and published a *NATPA Bulletin* (Chinese American Librarians Association 1995:17–18; Lai 1996:50). Other locales may put forth their own local flyers or newsletters. The national organization also issues a *NATPA Newsletter* four to six times a year and a *NATPA Forum* publication in English that comes out irregularly.

Given the large numbers of Taiwanese Americans who are employed in the science and technology fields, it should not be surprising that they also have their professional societies. For example, in 1991, an Association of Taiwanese Engineers in North America or *Taiwan Gongchengshi Xiehui* was formed to represent the interests of Taiwanese engineers in the United States. They present forums and talks but also have social activities for their members (Lai 1996:52).

Many Taiwanese professionals are in the health field. They graduated from medical schools in Taiwan such as those at National Taiwan University, National Tsing Hua University, Kaohsiung Medical College (*Gaoxiong Yixueyuan*), and the National Defense Medical College (*Guofang Yixueyuan*). These doctors can affiliate with regional chapters of the North American Taiwanese Medical Association (NATMA), an organization with its headquarters in University Park, Pennsylvania, that was founded in 1984 and publishes a *NATMA Journal* in English and Taiwanese. It puts out a newsletter at irregular intervals and claims that it has twelve hundred members across the United States. Its chapters try to work at the local level with medical and dental associations to aid in the professional growth, development, and advancement of their members. As many received their education and training in Taiwan, they are interested in ending discriminatory policies that are directed towards foreign medical and dental graduates. At the same time, they want to maintain links with their counterparts in Taiwan (Chinese American Librarians Association 1995:17).

"The chief business of the American people is business," said President Calvin Coolidge in a speech before the American Society of Newspaper Editors in 1925. But Taiwanese Americans are also very interested in business. Taiwanese Americans who are engaged in business can affiliate with local chapters of the Federation of Taiwanese Chambers of Commerce in North America (*Beimei Taiwan Shanghui Lianhehui*). Besides addressing the business interests of its membership and offering opportunities for networking, this organization tries to promote ties between Taiwan and the United States. In 1995, it had twenty-three branches in North America (Lai 1996:52). Local chapters of the organization may issue their own newsletters as well. Thus, the Chicago chapter issues a bimonthly *TACC Newsletter*. It also conducts monthly meetings to acquaint members with insurance, taxes, law, finance, marketing, international trade, and other relevant issues (Chinese American Librarians Association 1995:25).

Aside from the Taiwanese chambers of commerce, more specialized business and occupational associations have been formed. For example, there is a Taiwanese Innkeeper Association of Southern California (TIASC). Formed in 1974, it includes Taiwanese owners of motels, hotels, and inns. Its members often operate units belonging to lodging chains such as the Holiday Inn, Best Western, Comfort Inn, and Days Inn. They hold an annual meeting to discuss matters of common interest and arrange for discounts and benefits for their members, such as services and lower prices or charges from suppliers, accountants, lawyers, and bankers (Tseng 1994:126). More recently, a Taiwanese American Hotel/Motel Association was formed in 1989 with somewhat similar objectives.

Because of their familiarity with Asia, Taiwanese immigrants are in an excellent position to conduct international trade. Predictably then, a Taiwanese Import and Export Association (TIE) was established in 1989. With headquarters in New York City, it tries to promote a positive image of Taiwanese business people in the United States and elsewhere. In its membership are businesses ranging from industry and garment factories to food and jewelry stores. Each month it invites a prominent Taiwanese business person or politician to speak at its meetings. It also offers scholarships to students who contribute in some noteworthy way to the Taiwanese community.

Southern California with its large Taiwanese population has many other specialized organizations. Thus, there is a Southern California Chinese Computer Association (SCCCA). Founded in 1990, it includes a number of Chinese computer firms in Southern California, many of which are Taiwanese owned. This is not surprising, for Taiwan is a major manufacturer of computer products. In fact, it is the world's leading producer of monitors, modems, keyboards, scanners, and other computer parts or accessories. The Southern California Chinese Computer Association tries to get benefit packages for its members. This might pertain to business credit information, collection services, telecommunications, air express service, and lower prices from wholesalers. If problems of any sort arise, the association can try to apply pressure collectively to secure a more favorable outcome.

Recent arrivals from Taiwan may not know about the accepted practices and regulations in the conduct of business in America. Or there may be those who have worked for some time as computer scientists, engineers, chemists, or in another field who wish to start their own businesses or enterprises. For these people, there is an Organization of Chinese Entrepreneurial Advisory Networks (OCEAN) to provide mentoring and consulting information for members who may need assistance. In addition, there is a Chinese American Construction Association (CCACA), a Chinese American Scientists and Engineers Association, an Association of Taiwanese American Accountants, and an Association of Taiwanese American Attorneys (Tseng 1994:128–130; Lai 1996:52).

An example of a meeting by one of these groups would be that of the North American Taiwanese Engineers' Association (NATEA). It held a meeting on April 18, 1997, at a hotel in San Jose with a dinner and lecture. The organization had been formed in 1991, and at its meeting there would be a lecture by Dr. Yuan-tse Lee (Li Yuanze), the Nobel Prize winner in chemistry in 1986. The topic of his talk was "Science and Technology in Academia Sinica and Beyond" (*World Journal* 4/12/97:B6).

Political Organizations

Among the Taiwanese, there is a wide array of political organizations. Some focus on the politics of the Taiwan, while others focus on U.S. politics. Many of the groups concerned with the internal politics of Taiwan favor a loosening of Nationalist Party and Mainlander control of Taiwan. One group that deals with the political situation of Taiwan is the World United Formosans for Independence (WUFI), which was formed in 1970. Its headquarters are in Dallas, Texas, and it has many chapters in the United States, but it also maintains links with branches in Taiwan, Japan, Europe, Canada, South America, and elsewhere. Its purpose is to promote Taiwan as an independent and democratic country, a Republic of Taiwan that is free from China. It is active in holding talks and meetings and publishes the *Taiwan Tribune* (*Taiwan Gonglunbao*) to publicize this goal.

Another political organization is the Formosan Association for Public Affairs (FAPA). Headquartered in Washington, D.C., it was founded in 1982 and had thirty-nine chapters throughout the United States in 1996. It tries to keep a close watch on the U.S. Congress and to monitor legislation that might affect Taiwan. It also supports research on public policy and promotes education about Taiwan. In general, it is a lobbying network to promote human rights, democracy, and self-determination for Taiwan.

Lobbying is an important necessity for Taiwanese activists. The Center for Taiwan International Relations (CTIR), founded in 1988, has a rather similar aim. Also headquartered in Washington, D.C., it serves as a public policy center asserting that the sovereignty of Taiwan belongs to the Taiwanese. To further this goal, it organizes conferences, speakers, and research forums to shed light on the future of Taiwan. It also maintains an office in the Empire State Building in New York to work on issues in the United Nations that may affect Taiwan. This may include the question of Taiwan's gaining admission into the United Nations.

Still another political organization is the Formosan Association for Human Rights (FAHR). Founded in 1976, with its headquarters in Overland Park, Kansas, it works with Amnesty International to push for human rights in Taiwan. It puts out a *Taiwanese Human Rights Newsletter* in Taiwanese each month. The Taiwan International Alliance (TIA) also tries to promote human rights in Taiwan. Founded in 1992 by a noted feminist and politician from Taiwan, Xiulian Annette Lu, the organization attempts to make the international human rights community aware of happenings in Taiwan. It maintains offices in New York and Taibei and distributes a variety of different publications.

Since there are many students receiving an education at the college and university level, the *Taiwanese Collegian* targets this audience. Established in 1983, with its headquarters in Madison, Wisconsin, this is a national organization that works primarily with Taiwanese graduate students. It seeks to inform students about issues pertaining to Taiwan and to promote support for Taiwanese independence. It has affiliations with many of the major universities such as Cornell, Washington, Syracuse, Georgia Institute of Technology, Purdue, Kansas, Ohio State, Michigan, Texas A & M, Iowa State, and North Carolina State. Local groups at the different campuses invite speakers and organize other activities that relate to Taiwan. Each quarter the national organization also publishes the *Taiwanese Collegian* which had a circulation of three thousand in 1996.

For the Japanese community in America, there exists a civil rights organization known as the Japanese American Citizens League. For the Chinese community, there are two well-known civil rights organizations—the Chinese American Citizens Alliance (CACA) and the Organization of Chinese Americans (OCA). Immigrants from Taiwan have established a similar organization, the Taiwanese American Citizens League (TACL). Formed in Monterey Park in 1985, it became a national organization in 1989 with twelve chapters throughout the United States in 1996. Some of these chapters were in New York, New Jersey, Atlanta, Houston, and Seattle. The organization was most strongly represented in California, where there were chapters located in San Francisco, San Diego, and Los Angeles.

The Taiwanese American Citizens League tries to promote a sense of pride in being Taiwanese American. At the same time, it promotes good citizenship along with an awareness of the Taiwanese American heritage. It tries to join with other Taiwanese American organizations to address issues that affect the welfare of Taiwanese Americans. It has also attempted to have Taiwanese counted as a separate category by the U.S. Census. To further these aims, the organization supports a political internship program, summer and winter leadership camps, voter registration drives, seminars, community service involvement, and social events. Some chapters also offer scholarships for meritorious students. It also publishes an annual *Bulletin* and a newsletter in English and Taiwanese. Local chapters may likewise distribute a local newsletter or circular for their members.

The purposes of the Taiwanese organizations are not always clearly delineated into neat categories. They may have several objectives at the same time. A good example would be the Taiwanese Association of America. Originally formed to promote the interests and welfare of the Taiwanese community in the United States, it also sought to foster an appreciation for the heritage and culture of the Taiwanese. But in the 1970s, the organization became increasingly critical of the control of Taiwan by the Nationalist Party (*Guomindang*). Only after martial law was ended on Taiwan in 1987 did relations begin to improve between the Taiwan government and the Taiwanese Association of America (Lai 1996:51).

A caveat should also be noted. The Taiwanese do not join only Taiwanese organizations. They may join organizations with Chinese from Hong Kong, Singapore, Southeast Asia, and China. At the same time, whether they live in a community that has a few or many Taiwanese, they may also join non-Chinese organizations. Thus, they may be members of the local Chamber of Commerce, the Kiwanis Club, the Rotary Club, the Lions Club, Toastmasters International, and other professional or business groups.

Cultural Groups

As with any community, there can be a diversity of interests. This is indeed the case with the Taiwanese who have a wide variety of groups that one may join for fun and leisure. For those who enjoy singing, there are always chorus groups. Among the immigrant generation from Taiwan, choral singing is very popular. The groups include both men and women who sing favorite Chinese and Taiwanese folk songs. Often accompanied by a pianist, Taiwanese mixed chorus performances are a regular feature of many community celebrations. In some numbers, they will even dress up in folk costumes to appear like farmers, peasants, and fishermen. For other numbers or on special occasions, they will be dressed in formal attire.

For those whose interests lie in another direction, the options are opera groups or musical societies. If they wish, they can join together in a club to sing and even perform classical Chinese opera. That can be of the Beijing or several other regional Chinese varieties, such as the Taiwanese opera. Members can take turns singing the songs and performing the roles, although age, gender, and skill are important considerations as to the roles one can assume. Another possibility is to band together in a musical society. The members can play Chinese musical instruments such as the zither (*qin*), harp (*zheng*), a two-stringed violin (*erhu*), lute (*pipa*), flute (*xiao*), and so on. Sometimes the opera societies will also have members playing Chinese instruments to perform the opera songs. There are also studios and schools to teach traditional Chinese dance.

In recent years, karaoke has become extremely popular. An electronic innovation pioneered in Japan, it quickly spread to Hong Kong, Taiwan, Singapore, and the rest of Asia. It has also diffused into the United States. The karaoke equipment can supply the music, while people can supply the voices, trying to imitate famous singers or performers. With karaoke, there can be group participation or individual artistry in trying to sing songs. The karaoke can also supply the musical accompaniment for Chinese opera group performers. While clubs have opened to cater to this interest, karaoke groups have also been formed.

For those who are interested in exercise, there are groups and schools for martial arts, *taijiquan*, and *qigong*. Martial arts from Asia have become very popular as sports in the United States, having become even more well known because of action movies starring heroes such as Bruce Lee and Jackie Chan. Alongside the Japanese and Okinawan forms such as judo, jujitsu, aikido, kendo, and karate, there is the Filipino variety known as *escrima*. The Chinese version is known as *gongfu*, but Taiwanese children may learn the Chinese or Japanese forms. Belonging to a school means learning to take discipline and show respect for the teacher or *shifu*.

In many respects, Taiwan itself has become a hybrid model of American society. Because of the vast ties through immigration, education, business, and international relations, many U.S. cultural practices have been imported into Taiwan. People in Taiwan can play on golf courses or tennis and basketball courts in Taibei. Or they can engage in ballroom dancing. Among the Taiwanese Americans, there are groups devoted to golf, tennis, bridge or mahjong, and ballroom dancing. One can also find musical societies, opera groups, literary discussion societies, karaoke singing groups, and even informal eating groups dedicated to sampling various cuisines. The opportunities to affiliate with a cultural or recreational group are many, although one can also be a couch potato and just watch television and entertainment transmitted from Taiwan.

NEWSPAPERS AND THE MEDIA

Enter a Chinese supermarket, bookstore, or grocery, and one can easily see stands displaying a variety of Chinese language newspapers. Newspapers are an important resource to the Taiwan immigrant community for several reasons. First of all, they are a key means of providing information to this community in the United States. As many of the immigrants from Taiwan are of the first generation, a considerable number of them prefer to read Chinese language newspapers. Second, the papers help to sponsor events such as lectures, social activities, cultural events, and other happenings in the Taiwanese and Chinese community. In this way, they demonstrate that they are good corporate citizens with a sense of civic responsibility. Lastly, they help to make the non-Chinese community more aware of the presence of Taiwanese and Chinese in the United States. As the reporters from the Chinese papers seek interviews with political leaders and others, they also acquaint these individuals with the reality of a Chinese American community.

History of Chinese Papers in the United States

Chinese newspapers have a long history in the United States. From the earliest Chinese communities, newspapers have appeared to provide information that was important to them. The *Golden Hills' News*, for example, appeared in California as early as 1854. Along with the *The Oriental* in 1855 and the *Chinese Daily News* in 1857, these were the pioneers in the Chinese American press. But because of the small numbers of Chinese, the lack of literacy, and the problems of securing a stable income, these papers did not last long. Others arose to replace them, but their length of publication was usually also limited (Lai 1987:28).

During the nineteenth century, politics in China resulted in the development of both a reformist and a revolutionary faction. The reformist group favored the adoption of a constitutional monarchy, thereby retaining the legacy of China's system of emperors and dynasties. Reformers such as Kang Youwei felt that this lent continuity to the Chinese polity and was very similar to the Japanese example of an emperor with a Meiji constitution. On the other hand, the revolutionaries with their leader Sun Yatsen advocated a break with the past, ending imperial rule and forming a Chinese republic.

This vigorous debate was mirrored in the Chinese newspapers in the United States. Some papers were in favor of a constitutional monarchy and backed the reform faction. These included papers such as the *Wenxing Bao* in San Francisco and the *Xin Zhongguo Bao* in Honolulu. Others, however, openly championed the idea of a republic and backed Sun Yatsen. In San Francisco, the *Chung Sai Yat Po* (*Zhongxi Ribao*) at first adopted a reformist stance and later became more of a revolutionary paper (Ma 1990:88–89, 96–98).

The papers did not only inform about events in China, but they also pushed for changes in the Chinese community in the United States. Ng Poon Chew (Wu Panzhao) was a notable example. A newspaper editor and a Christian minister, he came to support Sun Yatsen. At the same time, he was a reformer who wanted to eliminate various antiquated habits among the Chinese in this country. He wanted to improve the welfare of the Chinese community even as he fought against anti-Chinese discrimination and legislation (Hoexter 1976).

Newspapers and the Taiwanese Community

Today the Chinese press continues to play an important role in the Taiwanese and Chinese community. The contrast to Chinese newspapers in the past—for example, those in the 1940s and 1950s—is that now there is more coverage of the Taiwanese community in the United States. As the Taiwanese community has grown since the 1960s, the Chinese newspapers seek its advertising business and have sought to expand their readership by acknowledging this group in their midst. More news coverage is therefore devoted to the Taiwanese living in the United States and not just the Cantonese.

The Chinese newspapers can be divided into three categories: national, regional, and special interest papers. The national papers are those with national distribution. They are affiliated with newspapers in Taiwan and Hong Kong and have a nationwide readership in this country. However, they maintain regional news bureaus and offices and put out regional or local editions. Prime examples would be the *World Journal* (*Shijie Ribao*), a Taiwan-affiliated paper, and the *Sing Tao Daily* (*Xingdao Ribao*), which is affiliated with Hong Kong. The *China Press* (*Qiao Bao*), on the other hand, is linked to China. Some papers like the *International Daily News* (*Guoji Ribao*) have a national edition but do not put out much in the way of regional coverage (Lai 1990; Y. Chen 1995).

The regional papers are those with limited distribution. Examples are the *Chinese Times* (*Jinshan Shibao*) in San Francisco, the *Seattle Chinese Post* (*Xihua Bao*) in Seattle, and the *United Chinese Press* (*Zhonghua Xinbao*) in Honolulu. These papers cater to a local clientele and therefore show a regional orientation. Their advertisements, news coverage, and smaller size all reflect a smaller base in advertising and readership. While a few are printed daily, others are printed only weekly. In recent years, the regional papers have encountered fierce competition from the national papers, which are vying for their business advertisers and newspaper readers. As a result, some of them have difficulty in surviving. An example might be the *Tribune* (*Luntan Bao*), a weekly paper that was published from Montebello, California, a suburb near Los Angeles in the 1980s but no longer exists.

The special interest papers do not have as wide a scope in news coverage as the national or regional papers. One example are the religious publications. Thus, the *Tzu Chi World Journal* (*Ciji Shijie*), a bilingual publication in Chinese and English, reports about the worldwide and U.S. activities of the Buddhist Compassion Relief Foundation. A number of other Taiwanese Buddhist organizations also publish papers for their followers. Another example are the Taiwanese independence publications. A paper such as the *Taiwan Tribune* (*Taiwan Gonglun Bao*) reports primarily on international events and political news that relate to the formation of a separate Republic of Taiwan. Its pages discuss the case for the distinctiveness of Taiwanese culture and language, apart from that of China. It also informs readers about the social activities of Taiwanese organizations that are sympathetic to its point of view.

Another category of special interest papers are the ones that are directly linked to the governments of Taiwan and China. The *Central Daily News* (*Zhongyang Ribao*) is seen as representing the official views of the Republic of China and the *People's Daily* (*Renmin Ribao*) as the official voice of the People's Republic of China. Both are considered government papers and news about the Chinese or Taiwanese in the United States is not carried regularly in their pages. An interesting point is that the *People's Daily* uses regular Chinese characters in its North American edition as a concession to its U.S. readers. In China and elsewhere, it uses the simplified Chinese characters.

Several of the key papers in the United States are linked to Taiwan. For example, the newspaper with the largest U.S. newspaper circulation is the

Chinese Daily News or *World Journal*, which is affiliated with media magnate Tih-wu Wang (Wang Tiwu) of Taiwan and the *United Daily News* (*Lianhe Bao*) of Taibei. Since its initial publication in 1976, the paper has expanded rapidly in the United States. According to one account, its circulation in the United States and Canada was about three hundred thousand at newstands in 1996 (*New York Times* 3/24/96:19).

The paper is the most successful of them all. It has several West Coast editions. For example, there is one edition for the Washington and Hawaii region, and one for the East Coast and New York region. There is one for the Northern California region and another for the Southern California region. It employs an enterprising set of reporters who actively solicit news for publication for each of the regions, who give their names for the bylines, and note the geographical origins of the stories. This willingness to have regional editions is a way of preempting local competition. It also assures the paper of a large demographic base to attract such advertisers as national life insurance companies, national telephone companies, and Wall Street brokerage firms.

Desirous of presenting the latest news, it draws from a wide variety of sources. For example, it makes use of a number of wire services like the Associated Press (AP), United Press International (UPI), and Reuters and subscribes to several newspaper services. Its pages frequently carry translations of news stories from major papers like the *New York Times*, the *Los Angeles Times*, and the *Washington Post*. It also features stories from magazines and periodicals such as *Time*, *Newsweek*, and *U.S. News and World Report*. In addition, it receives information by satellite transmission from Taiwan.

Because of the modernization and economic success of Taiwan and Hong Kong, the Chinese newspapers are able to implement the latest technology. Issues of the *World Journal*, *Sing Tao Daily*, or the *International Daily News* make many U.S. papers look dull and drab by comparison. For example, the *World Journal*, which is published daily, always sports colorful front and back pages for each newspaper section with bright red, yellow, green, blue, and pink. The words in Chinese characters and English words are printed in all colors, including basic black. The photographs on the front and back pages are in color, too. The Sunday paper may have seventy-five to eighty pages; the daily paper, more than sixty.

The *World Journal* has tremendous resources because of its ties to the *United Daily News* media empire in Taiwan. Not only does it have many regional offices and editions in the United States, but it has opened up many *World Journal* bookstores throughout the country. These stores display a wide

A *World Journal* Bookstore in Cupertino, California. Courtesy of Polly Lo.

variety of magazines, periodicals, and books in the Chinese language. The printed materials are about movie stars, history, women, current affairs, history, biography, literature, intellectual trends, and other themes. The *World Journal* also permits its readers to order magazines and books through its pages. A perusal of its issues reveals advertisements touting new books written by Buddhist leaders, politicians, or notable persons that can be obtained with the order forms it conveniently provides.

Coverage in Chinese Language Newspapers

Much like the average U.S. newspaper, the Sunday edition of the *World Journal* is the biggest and the thickest. It is divided into four sections, with the first one reporting international and national news along with sports. A second section offers regional news, while the third reports about notable people such as movie and television stars. A fourth is similar to a features, culture, and fashion supplement. In all the sections there are advertisements, news shorts, financial news, classified ads, announcements, and useful or interesting information.

In many ways, the coverage within a Chinese newspaper such as the *World Journal* can be an index to the concerns and interests of its reading public.

For example, the international news section reports events of interest happening around the world. The key stories appearing in a U.S. newspaper's front page or the nightly television news broadcasts are likely to be represented here. Most of the items, however, pertain to Taiwan, China, and Hong Kong. There are separate pages devoted to Taiwan, Hong Kong, China, and Southeast Asia. Politics, diplomacy, and current events receive a great deal of attention, especially the relations between Taiwan and China.

The national news coverage often focuses on the President, the Congress, and the military. Important pronouncements on economic and domestic policy are often noted. The positions of the two major political parties, the Republicans and the Democrats, are usually mentioned. As a result, an immigrant from Taiwan or China can learn about the twists and turns of U.S. politics quite quickly. Key natural disasters like floods and earthquakes are described, often accompanied by photographs.

For the regional editions, the news is appropriate to the geographical area. The Hawaii/Washington edition of the *World Journal*, for example, focuses on news in those two states. Coverage on what is happening in California is somewhat reduced. The Northern California edition, on the other hand, does not cover as much on those two states but devotes a great deal of attention to news and activities in the San Francisco Bay area and San Jose. The Southern California edition mostly focuses on the Los Angeles area, and news about San Francisco is very limited. Perhaps reflecting the cost of shipping it via airmail, the Hawaii edition in terms of pages is only one-third the length of the Northern California edition.

The regional reports include relevant news on state, county, and municipal levels. Thus, coverage will be found about the governor, the state legislature, mayors, city councils, and county governments. Prominent Chinese Americans and Asian Americans are certain to receive some interviews and publicity. Subjects such as social services, crime, education, health care, and transportation that affect the lives of the readership are reported. News about zoning changes, urban planning, or businesses that might affect neighborhoods also receive some attention. Visitors from Taiwan, Hong Kong, and China, especially those from sister cities to U.S. counterparts, are also likely to be the subject of stories.

Because many of the Taiwanese are in business, the papers devote a great deal of space to financial news. Business news about the United States, Europe, and especially Taiwan, Hong Kong, and China, is provided. In addition, the exchange rates of the currencies for different countries are supplied. Since some of the Taiwanese still have economic ties with their former homeland, a listing of Taiwan stocks and their losses or gains are detailed. Investment information on how construction, transportation, manufacturing, banking, and energy companies are doing is printed on a routine basis.

The classified advertisements and employment section in the paper give a clue to the occupations of the immigrants from Taiwan. Computer specialists, engineers, and accountants are in high demand. It is not only employers and businesses in this country that seek employees, but firms in Taiwan are also actively recruiting Taiwanese Americans. They want the Taiwanese Americans to work for their operations here in the United States or in Taiwan. The ads are in Chinese and may specify that an ability to speak Chinese and English is desirable.

Due to the rapid growth of the Chinese and Taiwanese population in the United States, many other types of employment opportunities are available. People for sales positions, insurance, financial planning, advertising, marketing, bookkeeping, and accounting are all needed. Office managers, supervisors, secretaries, receptionists, cooks, and travel agents are also sought. Other advertisements offer business opportunities such as restaurants, franchises, stores, and rental properties.

Besides being a source of helpful information, the papers have other features to attract a wide readership. The coverage of sports, movie stars and prominent personalities, and entertainment all serve that purpose. The Chinese language papers' sports sections report on football, basketball, baseball, tennis, golf, and figure skating. During the Olympics, the Asian games, and other major competitions, the coverage can be quite extensive. Chinese Americans such as tennis star Michael Chang, ice skater Michelle Kwan, and Olympic gymnast Amy Chow are given full coverage along with photographs. The extensive sports coverage suggests that Chinese readers are as interested in the subject as other Americans.

The section on movie and television stars and notable personalities is a popular part of the paper. There are separate pages for the movie stars and personalities from Taiwan, Hong Kong, and China. U.S. movie stars and personalities are not ignored on the front page. Like so many of the Hollywood glamour magazines, the papers discuss new movies or shows being produced in Hong Kong or Taiwan or China. Special joint productions with China or Japan or the United States are recognized. Rising singing stars and their place on the pop charts are noted. Those on performing tours and those attending festivals or fundraising events in dressy outfits are fully reported in the entertainment pages. The pairing with new boyfriends or girlfriends, divorces, marriages, and birthdays all receive the spotlight treatment.

The features section provides a mixed variety of articles to appeal to the newspaper's readership. Typically some pieces will deal with Chinese history,

Newspapers and magazines on display at a store.
Courtesy of Polly Lo.

culture, literature, or folklore. Famous Chinese rulers or persons such as the poets Li Bai (Li Bo) or Tao Qian are written up in biographical essays. At different times of the year, as festivals or commemorations are about to take place, the origins of the observance will be discussed and the symbolism of the event will be analyzed. Chinese New Year and the Mid-Autumn Festival, in particular, always receive a great deal of coverage.

But the features are not only about history and culture. Because the family is important, space is always devoted to domestic issues. Thus, there are discussions about the proper rearing of children and strategies for educational success. Brief essays and poems submitted by children are a regular part of the *World Journal*. Articles about achieving success in high school and preparing for college are standard fare. Recipes for various dishes and holiday foods for festive occasions are also to be found. Practical information about mutual funds, wills, financial planning, and handling taxes has been offered from time to time. In recent years, individuals from various walks of life have been asked to contribute their opinions on topics such as "Intermarriage," "What Should be the Relationship of Taiwan to China?" and "Should Immigrants Naturalize for Citizenship?"

Few newspapers seek an exclusively Taiwanese readership. To do so would restrict the pool of interested businesses who desire the widest audience possible for their advertisements. At the same time, the number of Taiwanese in the United States, while considerable, is not substantial enough in most parts of the country to be able to support papers that cater exclusively to them. As a result, the overwhelming majority of papers are Chinese papers that seek readers from Taiwan, Hong Kong, China, and Chinese from Southeast Asia. In this sense, the papers are like many of the ads in which insurance agents, real estate agents, financial planners, accountants, car dealers, and lawyers declare that they can speak English and different dialects of Chinese such as Mandarin Chinese, Taiwanese, Hakka, Cantonese, and Chaozhou (Teochiu). Nonetheless, readers from Taiwan are likely to prefer papers that are associated with Taiwan, such as the *World Journal* or *International Daily News.* Those from Hong Kong favor the *Sing Tao Daily* while some Chinese Americans like the *Chinese Times.* Immigrants from China are likely to buy the *China Press.*

The Politics of Chinese Newspapers

The Chinese language newspapers represent a wide array of political viewpoints. These include those that are sympathetic to China or to Taiwan and those that try to maintain a neutral stance. Relatively few side with China, especially after Beijing suppressed dissidents in the Tiananmen Incident of June 4, 1989. Most of the papers have historically supported Taiwan and its Nationalist Party. Those that have tried to maintain a nonpartisan, neutral position are the next largest bloc and include papers such as the *Chinese Times* of San Francisco and the *Sing Tao Daily.*

The fact that many papers support Taiwan has not prevented them from presenting a great deal of information about China. Several factors may account for this. One is that the readers are interested in news about China. China is a major political, military, and economic power in Asia, and the public wishes to be informed about current events as they relate to it. A second is that the United States has formal diplomatic relations with China and does not formally recognize Taiwan. As a result, it is somewhat awkward to ignore Chinese diplomats who attend functions at the United Nations in New York, meet with the World Bank, or deal with the U.S. Department of State in Washington, D.C. In short, the relations between China and the United States are so extensive that many Taiwanese Americans are involved in business dealings with Beijing.

On the other hand, Taiwan's relations with the United States are not neglected. The activities of the local or regional office of the Taibei Economic and Cultural Centers in San Francisco, Los Angeles, Houston, New York, Chicago, or Honolulu are widely reported in the Chinese language papers. Although Taiwan is not formally recognized by the United States, the head personnel at these offices are equivalent to consuls general or consuls. They are active in the Chinese and Taiwanese communities in the United States, often appearing at social functions and community events. They attend summer picnics, visit Chinese language schools, host beauty pageants, and honor business and community leaders. They also offer donations to certain causes and help subsidize some cultural performances. Touring youth and performing groups, as well as the corporate presence of Taiwanese businesses like China Airlines, often contribute to the cultural life of many communities.

News coverage of the papers supporting Taiwan has changed somewhat because of the internal politics of the island itself. In recent years, with the end of martial law and the rivalry among different political parties in Taiwan, the papers do not report only about the dominant Nationalist Party or *Guomindang*. Other parties such as the New Party (*Xindang*), the Democratic Progressive Party (*Minjindang*), and the Taiwan Independence Party (*Jianguodang*) have appeared to challenge the Nationalist Party. The political developments in Taiwan have become increasingly complex, and the papers report the debates and maneuvering by the different parties as they vie for power. These contests have a certain immediacy as politicians from the different parties occasionally visit the United States to explain their positions and to ask for support and donations from the Taiwanese community.

The newspapers can provide a glimpse of nationalism, transnationalism, and other perspectives. In recent years, the papers have reported about anger at Japan's failure to come to terms with its responsibility for its role in Asia during World War II. Japan's occupation of the Diaoyutai islands, also known as the Senkaku islands, has also elicited indignation. Demonstrations in Taiwan and among Taiwanese Americans have occurred over these two issues. In Taiwan, too, there was vast concern about letting its national treasures from the National Palace Museum be sent abroad for display in American museums. They were to be part of a touring "Splendors of Imperial China" exhibit in 1996, but the Taiwanese saw them as an irreplaceable part of their national and cultural patrimony.

Even as the people in Taiwan wrestle with the questions of their identity as Chinese, Taiwanese, or both, other complex issues are examined for their possible relevance. Should Tibet be allowed autonomy or independence from China? Does Taiwan's hosting the Dalai Lama have any implications for China? Is Taiwan like Quebec in Canada? Or is it like the two Koreas and the two Germanies, prior to the latter's reunification? Or should Taiwan see itself like an Israel that was formed despite sentiment against its formation as an independent nation? These and many other political questions are often treated in the pages of the newspapers.

In addition to reporting about developments in Taiwan, Hong Kong, and China, the Chinese language papers follow closely issues that affect Chinese Americans and Asian Americans. When legislation, laws, or measures have the potential to affect immigration policy or immigrants, the newspapers discuss their possible impact upon the Chinese American or Asian American communities. Matters affecting neighborhoods, the elderly, education, health, and public safety are closely monitored. Issues that appear to be discriminatory or might have an adverse effect upon the readership are likely to receive intense coverage. Editorials may discuss important developments and analyze their consequences for the Chinese American community. In general, the papers are in favor of empowering the Chinese American and Asian American populations.

Reflecting an awareness that their readership may not be as conversant in English as they might wish, the papers even include language lessons. Translations of idiomatic expressions or colloquialisms into Chinese are common with examples to show how the English phrase should be used. On occasion, statements or comments by leaders or prominent persons are presented in both Chinese and English, so that readers can see what famous people have said in a public speech or address. For parents who want their children to learn Chinese, these lessons could presumably also be used to teach them how to translate English expressions.

The newspapers are also patrons of Chinese community events—lectures, forums, art exhibitions, book displays, and other cultural activities. While this helps to validate their status as good corporate citizens, it is also good marketing and public relations. Partly to cement ties with their readers, they subsidize community functions that have great interest and high visibility. Thus, for example, the *World Journal* has occasionally sponsored Chinese opera performances and concerts. When the paper does help support such activities, its pages give them prominent display. Large type and photographs help generate special interest and catch the reader's eye.

Although the press plays an important role within the Taiwanese and Chinese community, it assumes another function with others. With its reporters interviewing politicians and others, the Chinese press helps to publicize the community. Its presence promotes awareness of the Chinese community as a force to be reckoned with. Public figures become more cognizant of the Taiwanese and Chinese population as voters or consumers. When the *World Journal* celebrated its twentieth anniversary of publishing in the United States in 1996, a special issue was filled with congratulations. Among the well-wishers were Governors Pete Wilson of California and George Pataki of New York and Premier Michael D. Harris of Ontario, Canada. Mayors Willie Brown of San Francisco and Susan Hammer of San Jose were but a few of the many public dignitaries who extended their congratulations (*World Journal* 2/12/96:D1–2).

In addition to the newspapers, other print media are available to the Taiwanese and Chinese communities. Bookstores, supermarkets, and stores display magazines, periodicals, books, and comic books catering to every interest. The sources of these publications are Taiwan, Hong Kong, China, Singapore, and the United States. In major U.S. cities such as Los Angeles, San Francisco, New York, and Honolulu, occasional bookfairs and expositions are held so that the public can see the great assortment of publishing materials that are available in Chinese. Devoted bibliophiles can linger to their hearts' content and browse through a huge inventory that normally is not found easily in ordinary bookstores. Noted authors make appearances and autograph books. The sponsors of these well-publicized events include various book companies, bookstores, newspapers, and media-related businesses.

Other Media

In recent years, other media have become available as means of communication and entertainment. These include radio broadcasts, television, and the Internet. In a number of major cities, such as New York, Chicago, and Honolulu, radio programming is available in Cantonese and Mandarin Chinese. The broadcasts are usually restricted to certain days and certain hours, rather than having continuous air play, and the programming is a mix of music, news, and advertisements. In general the radio broadcasts have a limited audience and do not challenge the primacy of the newspapers.

Television. Much more popular and a real rival to the press are the television stations. This pattern is similar to what is happening in American society as a whole. Depending on the city, Chinese television programming may be available on regular stations and cable, or via satellite transmission. The television broadcasts are in Mandarin Chinese and Cantonese, the portion of each in part dependent upon the size of the listening base or the channel. Regular television channels usually broadcast at least several hours each day, their program time much more extensive than that of their radio counterparts. The viewing audience is also much larger, for television has a greater appeal to the Chinese community.

The television stations have a mixed fare. The news programs normally include local telecasts as well as satellite transmissions relayed from Hong Kong, Taiwan, and China. Beamed into homes, it allows viewers to see key figures or politicians being interviewed by television journalists just as the news event is occurring. Natural disasters—summer typhoons, floods, earthquakes, and so on—are telecast just as viewers in Asia would have seen them. The financial news about the stock markets in Hong Kong and Taiwan is reported daily, and one can learn about the general economic climate in Asia. Even the weather for Taiwan is reported, so that one can find out about the temperature for Taibei, Gaoxiong, or Tainan. A traveler who is making a brief trip can easily learn what to bring in terms of clothing.

Television viewers have a choice of varied programming. Besides the news, they can watch soap operas, martial arts action films, historical programs, contemporary dramas, and variety shows. Almost everything that is available on American television can also be found in a Chinese format. This includes talk shows, game shows, cooking programs, and cultural programs that discuss history, society, folklore, and societal practices. At one time, a historical drama featured a popular series about a famous magistrate and historical figure known as "Judge Bao (*Bao Qingtian*)." The Taiwan channel carried one version of this, while the Hong Kong channel simultaneously broadcast a different version. The same actor portrayed the lead character in both, but the plots had been scripted differently for the Cantonese and Taiwanese audiences.

The soap operas are also interesting to watch. Key characters, whom the public soon learns to love or hate, are developed. Innocence, intrigue, conspiracy, and betrayal are woven into the daily segments of these long-running serials that spin out complex plots and subplots. The characters often find themselves ensnared in situations that no one could foresee, but that can bring conflict, pain, and sorrow or reconciliation and love. The theme songs for the soap operas or historical and cultural programs sometimes become hot items for the pop song charts. Movie magazines and newspapers minutely follow the twists and turns of the actors' lives in these soap operas, both on and off the screen.

The talk shows deal with the political, cultural, or social issues of the day. Prominent politicians, for example, may be brought in to discuss pending legislation. Members of the different political parties, along with scholars, will offer their opinions about what is happening and the possible ramifications of the action. Alternatively, popular stars will appear and obtain publicity for a movie, television show, or song. Sometimes personalities from Hong Kong and China will mingle with those from Taiwan. There is a considerable amount of crossover in the entertainment world, for Hong Kong movie stars such as Jackie Chan (Cheng Long) and singing and acting star Andy Lau (Liu Dehua) are very popular in Taiwan.

During Chinese New Year or the Lunar New Year, the television channels will have special entertainment programs. People who have been in the news or entertainment superstars are featured during this time. A review of the past year, predictions for the coming one, and an accounting of the festivities to take place are part of the regular programming. The symbolism of cultural practices such as displays of oranges or spring couplets, or the preparation of holiday foods, are discussed with chefs or cooking teachers. Spring couplets are sayings bearing good wishes for the new year. Everyone shares hopes that the new year will bring good fortune and prosperity for all, and the screen is filled with expressions of cheer and wishes for good luck.

Movies and Videotapes. Whereas television provides both information and entertainment, movies and videotapes are much more purely for entertainment. Movie theaters feature films made in Hong Kong, Taiwan, and China. During the week, the audiences are small as everyone is working. But on weekends or holidays, the number of moviegoers will be much larger. Although renting videotapes would be much cheaper, those who go out to the movies enjoy the experience of a bigger screen. They can also sip cartons of soybean milk and nibble beef or pork jerky, cracked seeds, or other snacks sold at the counter. For several hours, they can savor an evening out of the house and mingle with other movie viewers.

The theaters usually present two different films at each performance. The movies shown fall into several categories. One type is the martial arts films, which can be in either a historical context or present context. The action heroes or heroines may demonstrate magical powers in some of these adventure movies. Another type is the police, hoodlum, and gambler movies. These plots include high-speed car chases, sting operations, and competing gangs. Still another category is the ghost stories. For a while, vampires were quite the rage, but that trend seems to have crested. Finally, there is the romance or love stories, which can also be vehicles for comedy.

In recent years, some film directors from Hong Kong, China, and Taiwan have enjoyed critical acclaim. The Chinese theaters show these films, which have also played in non-Chinese theaters, but many of the other presentations are best described as B- or C-grade movies. They are not of the variety shown at film festivals, but they provide comic relief or family enjoyment. The viewers want the diversion and the chance to see the actors that they have read or heard about in the print media. Some of the actors are also singers, so audiences may have listened to the songs or ballads sung by these stars. All the films have subtitles, so those who do not understand the Cantonese or Mandarin Chinese dialogue can still follow the plot.

For people who want another option, Chinese videostores can always be found. The assortment of films on videotapes they offer is much wider than that which can be shown in Chinese theaters. They stock the videotapes of movies that have been shown in Taiwan, Hong Kong, and China. Movies made for television, educational programs, and children's cartoons—even Japanese *manga* animated features—are on the shelves. Movies made in Hong Kong can be found dubbed in Mandarin Chinese, and those made in Taiwan can be found dubbed in Cantonese. At some videostores, depending upon the clientele served, Chinese movies may also be available in the Vietnamese, Thai, Lao, Cambodian, and Hmong languages.

Internet. As technology brings rapid changes, the modes of delivering information and entertainment are being dramatically transformed. The Internet has made it possible to communicate with people around the world through electronic mail. It is also possible to use the Internet to link up with different websites to access information. Colorful graphics, visual displays, and sound presentations are available on these websites as well.

For many Taiwanese Americans, adapting to this technology is relatively easy. Many of them are highly educated professionals, and they have already learned how to use computers. As a result, many are making skillful use of the Internet highway and accessing sites across the country and across the ocean in Taiwan, Hong Kong, and China. Some Chinese newspapers have created websites for readers, and the *China Times* is a popular site to read about developments in Taiwan. It is also possible for devoted fans to contact websites to access colorful photographs and personal information about the stars of television, film, and the recording industry that they admire.

Taiwanese organizations have eagerly embraced this new technology, so the Internet has a strong representation of Taiwanese groups, with a number of Taiwanese webservers and homepages for Taiwanese organizations. Thus, the Taiwanese American Citizens League (TACL), the Formosan Association for Public Affairs (FAPA), the Taiwanese Association of America (TAA), and the Hakka all maintain websites. Those who contact those sites can often choose to read the information and announcements in English or Chinese.

Taiwanese student organizations have been enthusiastic in responding to the Internet technology. Surfing the Internet soon reveals that the Taiwanese student associations at many major universities have set up websites, and one can view photographs of students eating together at a meal table or having fun at some activity. The students use the sites as a way to acquaint peers with their organization and invite them to join and participate. It also allows them to network with other clubs on different campuses and to collaborate in joint programs or to sponsor large conferences. In electronic mail communications, they can argue whether the island of Taiwan is shaped like a sweet potato, a yam, or a tobacco leaf or debate the sublime pleasures of chewing betel nuts, a traditional pastime in Taiwan—subjects they can also discuss in contacts with Taiwanese student associations in Canada, Australia, Japan, and Europe.

On the whole, the newspapers and the various forms of media are adaptive mechanisms that can help in the adjustment of immigrants from Taiwan. Even for those who read English language papers, the Chinese press and media provide an alternative or complementary source of information. U.S. newspapers and television programs simply do not have very good coverage of contemporary events in Taiwan and Asia. Moreover, by reading the Chinese newspapers or viewing the Chinese language television programs, members of the Taiwanese community can share common experiences and feel that they are maintaining connections with their cultural roots.

RELIGION

Ever since the immigration quota was enlarged in 1965, the United States has become an increasingly diverse mosaic. In a way, this is the reinventing of America, a theme which has occurred over and over again throughout its rich and complex history. As the immigrants and refugees arrive, they bring along with them their faiths and beliefs. They may therefore transplant religions that are compatible with their traditional values and culture. However, some may eventually alter the form of their beliefs and practices, while others may adopt new religious faiths.

Among the Taiwanese immigrants, the religious orientations can be quite diverse. There are those who subscribe to Christianity and those who favor the practices traditional in Taiwan. The latter consist of Buddhism, Daoism, Confucianism, and popular religion, which is a blend of ancestor worship, belief in local and city gods, and syncretism with Buddhism, Daoism, and Confucianism. But regardless of the religious orientation, the immigrants' beliefs can help them adapt to America. Like voluntary associations, religious groups can permit fellowship with others and give its members access to information and support. Religious groups can also affirm certain values and provide beliefs to sustain the faithful in their lives.

Chinese Religions

As the immigration from Hong Kong, Taiwan, China, and Southeast Asia has increased, Chinese religions have become more visible on the American landscape. For immigrants from Taiwan, this means that opportunities to practice Buddhism, Daoism, and Chinese popular religion are more readily available. The Buddhists of China, Taiwan, and Hong Kong are of the Mahayana school, which makes them similar to those from Japan, Korea, and Vietnam. Those from Laos, Cambodia, Thailand, Sri Lanka, and Myanmar are of the Theravada school. The ones from Tibet are of the Tantric Buddhism school.

Chinese Buddhist organizations and temples from Taiwan have enjoyed rapid growth in recent years. For example, there is a Xi Lai (Hsi Lai) Temple in Los Angeles, a Jade Buddha Temple in Houston, a Zhuangyen (Chuang Yen) monastery in New York, and a City of Ten Thousand Buddhas Temple in San Francisco. All of these, and many others, are all offshoots from Taiwan, where in recent years, Buddhism has been experiencing great popularity. Buddhists have increased from an estimated eight hundred thousand in 1983 to 4.9 million in 1995 (D. Lin 1996a:7). This is a sixfold increase even though the population has increased only 12 percent. Eager to share their beliefs, Buddhist organizations from Taiwan have now established many branches in the United States and other parts of the world.

The Xi Lai Temple at Hacienda Heights in Los Angeles is especially interesting. "Xi Lai" means "coming to the West." Located near Monterey Park, the temple is close to the largest concentration of Taiwanese in the world. It is affiliated with Foguangshan (Fo Kuang Shan) or "Buddha's Light Mountain," the largest Buddhist center in Taiwan. Its leader is Master Xingyun (Hsing Yun), who is the forty-eighth patriarch of the Linzhi school of Chan Buddhism. Chan Buddhism is better known to the West as Zen Buddhism. Foguangshan has many branches in Taiwan, but it has become international with more than a hundred temples throughout the world. In the United States, it has opened branches in San Francisco, New York, Dallas, Denver, San Diego, and elsewhere, but its largest overseas temple is the Xi Lai Temple in Los Angeles.

Occupying fifteen acres, the entire complex is a scaled-down version of its parent organization in Taiwan. Built at a cost of $26 million and completed in 1988, the complex looks like architecture that belongs in Taiwan or China.

The temple itself is large with stairs leading up to it. Its red columns and a yellow-tiled roof make it a colorful sight. Within the building are Buddhas, bodhisattvas, and other Buddhist statues; one hall has ten thousand golden Buddhas. Urns with burning incense give forth circling swirls of smoke, and in the background monks and nuns move about. The courtyard around the building is spacious and impressive, conveying a sense of awe and majesty.

On weekends, busloads of visitors come up to the red gate in front of the temple. In fact, the temple has become one of the most popular tourist attractions in Los Angeles, and guides speaking Chinese and English direct the crowds of tourists. Milling around and armed with cameras, some people have traveled here just to look at this spectacular temple, but many come as worshippers to light incense sticks, make offerings, and bow to pay their respects. Others visit for the vegetarian meals of tofu and other items served in its dining room. All can make donations to the temple.

Designed to handle a wide variety of activities, the temple includes classrooms, auditoriums, reception rooms for instruction and lectures on Buddhism, administrative offices, a library, a residence for monks and nuns, and a gift shop. Religious activities are offered on weekdays and on weekends, so the complex is always busy and teeming with people. But on holidays such as the Chinese New Year's Eve and New Year's Day, it is even more crowded.

Connected with the Xi Lai Temple or Foguangshan branches is the Buddhist Light International Association (BLIA). This is a lay organization that complements the monks and nuns of Foguangshan. It plans and sponsors activities that are not services handled by the monks and nuns. These are Dharma discussion groups, meditation classes, and lectures handled and organized by lay members, who also solicit donations and recruit new members. In any geographical area, when an interested group of individuals number about one hundred persons, they can petition to establish a new Buddhist Light International Association chapter. As of 1996, twenty-two chapters, nineteen subchapters, and five organizing communities existed in the United States (I. Lin 1996:112).

The Buddhist Compassion Relief Ziji (Tzu Chi) Foundation is another large Taiwan-based organization that has developed roots in the United States. Led by Master Zhengyen (Cheng Yen), it is headquartered at Hualian, a city in eastern Taiwan, has fifty-three offices in seventeen countries, and has many branches worldwide devoted to the teaching of Buddhist tenets. In the United States, it has groups of followers in Los Angeles, Houston, San Jose, New York, San Francisco, and Honolulu. Emphasizing relief and charity work for others, it publishes a colorful *Tzu Chi World Journal* (*Ziji Shijie*), a bilingual Chinese and English paper that reports on its activities.

By emphasizing charity and service, the Buddhist organizations such as Foguangshan and Ziji have infused their members with a sense of purpose. Ziji, for example, provides counseling, financial and emotional support for the distressed, health programs, international relief, and education. It has provided relief and assistance, such as food and supplies to the victims of the San Francisco earthquake in 1989, the Southern California wildfires in 1993, the Northridge earthquake in Southern California in 1994, and the Alaska flood victims in the same year. It operates a medical clinic and offers dental care provided by volunteer dentists. It has given scholarships to nursing students in South Central Los Angeles since 1990 ("Tzu Chi" 1997).

That the Buddhist presence is not restricted to the West Coast of the United States is symbolized by the Jade Buddha Temple in Houston and the Zhuangyen Monastery in New York. The Jade Buddha Temple in Houston is linked to the Texas Buddhist Association (TBA) in Houston, which has more than a thousand members. The organization was formed in 1987 and built its Jade Buddha Temple in 1990. The temple has a Grand Buddha Hall, a Guanyin Meditation Hall, and a youth activity center. It also has a library, cafeteria, residential areas, and a serene lotus pond. Among its many activities are meditation retreats, dharma talks, readings, discussions, and programs in the Chinese and English languages.

In New York, the Zhuangyen Monastery shows dramatically that Buddhism has also penetrated the Northeast. Located at Carmel, New York, the monastery is endowed with large grounds and many buildings. A Guanyin Hall is dedicated to the Bodhisattva Avalokitesvara. The Thousand Lotus Memorial Terrace has 1050 steel niches to hold the cremated remains of individuals in urns. The Hall of Ten Thousand Buddhas has the largest enclosed statue of the Buddha in the world. A thirty-seven foot statue of the Buddha Vairocana is encircled by ten thousand small statues of the Buddha on a lotus terrace. In addition, the monastery has a library, dining hall, activity center, living quarters, and a Seven Jewels Lake on the grounds.

The Zhuangyen Monastery is affiliated with the Buddhist Association of the United States (BAUS). Its followers reside in New York, New Jersey, and Connecticut. Its activities are diverse and include services, Sunday meditations, retreats, dharma talks, book discussion groups, and vegetarian luncheons. In May 1997, it scheduled a dedication of its hall with the enclosed Great Buddha. Representatives of Chinese, Korean, Japanese, Thai, and Tibetan Buddhist groups participated in the ceremonies and activities. The Dalai Lama was also expected to attend the event ("Chuang Yen" 1997).

Popular Religion

The popular religion of Taiwan is a syncretic mix of Buddhism, Daoism, and Confucianism. For many of its practitioners, it is not important to define the precise boundaries of what is Buddhist or what is Daoist. What does matter is that they believe in a complex of different gods and deities. In Taiwan, these include the God of the Earth (Tudigong), the Goddess of Mercy (Guanyin or the Bodhisattva Avalokitesvara), the Goddess of the Sea (Mazu or Tianhou), and the Buddha (Fozu). Others include the God of the North Pole Star (Xuantian Dadi), the Monk Qingshui Zushi, the God of War (Guangong), the City God (Chenghuangye), the God of Wealth (Cai-shenye), and the Maitreya Buddha (Milefo).

Many of these gods and deities of the popular religion in Taiwan are also subscribed to by the Cantonese. Thus, in various communities in the United States, temples to Guanyin and Mazu or Tianhou already exist. But with the arrival of Taiwanese immigrants, new temples are being built. In San Francisco, a Mazu Temple was started in 1986 by people from Taiwan. In addition to the altar and hall dedicated to Mazu, it has an activity center for lectures and meditation as well as for Chinese language lessons. In recent years, some Taiwanese Americans have made pilgrimages to Meizhou, an island off the mainland Chinese province of Fujian. Tradition has it that a woman from Meizhou later became the goddess Mazu.

While the activities of temples and study groups attract notice, many Taiwanese practice religion in the privacy of their homes. Buddhism, Daoism, and popular religion do not require weekly attendance at a church or temple. They do not demand congregational services or public gatherings. Instead, their beliefs are demonstrated in ancestor worship, events that pertain to rites of passage, festivals or community observances, and key happenings according to the Chinese lunar calendar. These practices are part of a continuum that link religion and folk practices or customs to their identity as Chinese or Taiwanese. This includes the consultation of Chinese almanacs, concerns about *yin-yang*, *fengshui*, divination, and taboos. As a result, even as Christians, Chinese and Taiwanese may subscribe to some practices tied to popular religion.

Christianity

Christianity came to Taiwan in the seventeenth century with the Europeans. The Dutch were Protestants, while the Spanish and Portugese were Catholics. Though they tried to convert the Chinese and aborigines, their

A Taiwanese Presbyterian Church in Southern California. Courtesy of Polly Lo.

efforts were stopped by the Ming loyalist Zheng Chenggong when his forces seized control of the island. In the nineteenth century, Presbyterians and Catholics settled in Taiwan to start missionary work. In this effort, the Presbyterians were more successful. They set up hospitals and schools and in 1885 even launched a newspaper that was printed in romanized Taiwanese (Rubinstein 1991:251–52).

Overall, though, in the nineteenth and twentieth centuries, Christian missionary efforts achieved only limited success. Gains won by Christians, especially the Protestants, were limited by the Japanese control over the island after the end of the Sino-Japanese War of 1894–95. This continued down until 1945 when World War II saw the defeat of the Japanese. From that point on conversion to Christianity registered steady growth until the 1960s and 1970s. Once dramatic economic expansion and prosperity occurred in Taiwan, its residents returned to their traditional religious practices and the growth of Christianity on the island leveled off. The people of Taiwan realized that Christianity was not a prerequisite for modernization and technological change (Rubinstein 1991:271–72).

In the United States, however, a greater percentage of Taiwanese attend Christian churches than in Taiwan. One reason is that a large portion of the Taiwanese immigrants were educated at a higher level and were Christians

A Chinese Evangelical Free Church in Los Angeles. Courtesy of Polly Lo.

even before they moved to America. A second reason is that Christian churches are also seen as places for fellowship and companionship. They are seen as immigrant or ethnic churches, and some Taiwanese do not care so much about the denomination as that they can be with other Taiwanese.

The denominations of Christianity that the Taiwanese subscribe to are often Protestant or Catholic. Most are Protestants, and they may be Southern Baptists, Presbyterians, Methodists, Congregationalists, Lutherans, Episcopalians, or Seventh Day Adventists. They may also be True Jesus Pentecostalists, Mormons, or members of the Assemblies of God or Holiness churches. All of these denominations are represented in Taiwan (Rubinstein 1991:271–72). Many Taiwanese, however, belong to Protestant churches that are nondenominational Baptist and are of the fundamentalist or evangelical variety. While some belong to churches that are not primarily Chinese in composition, others seek out churches that are. These individuals may prefer that the services are conducted in Mandarin Chinese or Taiwanese.

A number of Presbyterian churches offer services conducted in Mandarin Chinese. They may also have sermons in the Taiwanese or the Minnan dialect. In Taiwan, the Presbyterians chose to identify themselves with the Taiwanese and printed Bibles in Taiwanese romanization. The Presbyterian Church in Taiwan had also in the past supported Taiwanese dissidents against the Nationalist government (Tyson 1967:167). Because of this close association in Taiwan, some Taiwanese immigrants have maintained this affiliation in the United States. However, in many locales, Taiwanese Presbyterians are also willing to join other Taiwanese or Chinese Protestant churches.

The Taiwanese participate in churches that vary in size and membership. If the numbers of Taiwanese in a geographical area are not great, they use a school building or ask to use a non-Chinese church for their services. Or they join with a Chinese American church whose membership speaks primarily Cantonese and English. Once the population of Taiwanese or Mandarin-speaking Chinese increases, attempts are made to form a new church that can have services in Mandarin or Taiwanese. But because the composition of the Chinese may be so varied, there are usually also students and others from Hong Kong, China, Singapore, and Southeast Asia. These Chinese are eagerly recruited, for they can help to sustain the financial operations of the church. Unless there is a certain number of members, it will be difficult to pay for a pastor, the rent or mortgage payments for the church, the water and electricity bills, building repairs, church supplies, books, and other costs.

Many times, however, several Chinese churches will coexist in a town or city. There are several reasons for this. First, members of the several congregations prefer different mixes of English, Cantonese, Taiwanese, and Mandarin Chinese services. For example, one church may have a bilingual service while another may have a service in just one language. Another reason is that the manner of the pastor or the operating style of the board of deacons at one church may be more appealing to some than that at another. Securing a minister or pastor who is Chinese is not always possible. A third factor is the composition of the congregation. The number of American-born Chinese, Cantonese, Taiwanese, mainland Chinese, and non-Chinese congregants might influence the choice. The class or professional status of the congregation, as well as the age of the members, is also a consideration, as is the range of available activities. People wish to affiliate with those who have a similar background (Palinkas 1984:255–77).

Churches that include a mix of Chinese with different language backgrounds may have complicated meeting and activity schedules. One church, for example, had one Sunday worship service in Mandarin Chinese and Cantonese. Another service an hour and a half later, conducted in Mandarin Chinese and English, probably appealed more to the second-generation youth. There was also a Cantonese Fellowship, English Fellowship, Senior Citizen Fellowship, and an Asian Bible Study Group. The church's newsletter, however, was written entirely in Chinese.

Similar to most Christian churches, Taiwanese churches have a wide variety of activities. At a Sunday service, new visitors are introduced to the congregation. In addition to Sunday services, there are Bible study groups, prayer meetings, and lectures. The churches usually have a choir, women's group, Sunday school, youth group, and a board of deacons. Their social events include brunches, buffets, dinners, talks, trips, and programs for special occasions. During the summer, recreational programs, retreats, or camps are offered for the youth. In many cases, the churches will also offer Mandarin Chinese language classes. If there is a demand, the churches will schedule English instruction for newer immigrants (Palinkas 1984:260). At various times if conflicts do not occur, the churches will be made available for meetings or cultural performances by other community groups.

In Taiwanese church activities, women play an important role. They are the ones who attend the services most regularly. Concerned about family, they help to bring the youth to services and church functions. Finally, they are the core of volunteers who help to make family activities and social events an integral part of any functioning church. By preparing the food for potlucks, buffets, or dinners and tending to social activities, they insure that the churches will be hospitable and inviting places. Their presence and participation are indispensable for the success of the churches in the Taiwanese community.

At many colleges and universities, Taiwanese youth participate in Bible study groups. Depending on the ethnic composition of the campus or area, they have the option of joining Asian, Chinese, or Taiwanese Bible study groups. Stanford University, for example, has an Asian American Christian Fellowship (AACF) and a Chinese Christian Fellowship (CCF). The former includes different Asian American groups, while the latter is comprised of Chinese from Hong Kong, Taiwan, China, Southeast Asia, and elsewhere. Harvard University and Radcliffe College have both a Harvard-Radcliffe Asian American Christian Fellowship (HRAACF) and a Harvard-Radcliffe Christian Fellowship (HRCF). The latter group does not specifically target Asians. Membership in a Bible study group can affirm a sense of ethnic identity even as it also offers a universal identity based on faith (Busto 1996: 135, 138, 141).

Because they are away from home and their parents, students often find that these groups meet a spiritual need. They turn to these Protestant forms of evangelical Christianity for religion and direction. But they also welcome the fellowship and interaction of those who are of their own youth group and generation. Being rooted in these Bible study groups gives them a sense of focus and mission. They can make a commitment to something which they feel is intellectually and emotionally meaningful. Simultaneously they enjoy the company of others in prayer meetings, Bible studies, and social gatherings.

The Bible study groups can be locally based or affiliated with national organizations. Examples of nationally affiliated organizations are the Navigators, InterVarsity Christian Fellowship (IVCF), and Campus Crusade for Christ (CCC). Several campuses across the country have local chapters of the Asian American Christian Fellowship (AACF). This organization sees itself as Christian and nondenominational in its ministry. Many evangelical organizations are aware of the rapid growth of minorities in the United States. They know that Asian Americans represent a significant portion of that demographic growth. As a result, InterVarsity Christian Fellowship started a series of "ABC" (Asians, Blacks, and Chicanos) conferences in 1976. Likewise, Campus Crusade for Christ initiated an Intercultural Ministry in the mid-1970s. These organizations have also come to include large numbers of Asian Americans in their staff and ministry (Busto 1996:134–37).

The second-generation Taiwanese and Chinese may be taking a different path than their parents. Some observers note that the second generation feels much more comfortable with English language sermons and activities. They consider professional, class, and generational ties to be more important than the use of the Taiwanese or Mandarin Chinese languages. Overall, their interests are likely to be different than those of the first generation. On the other hand, the first-generation immigrants very much desire worship services using those languages. These different preferences mean that pastors and ministers have difficulty catering to the two audiences, and the younger graduates from theological seminaries and divinity schools, who are not bilingual, are more interested in working with the second-generation congregations. The result is that the first-generation immigrant churches do not find it easy to find pastors or ministers (Lee 1996:51). In a sense, as the Taiwanese community evolves so do the demands that they place on the churches in which they worship.

FESTIVALS

Most Taiwanese want to preserve their cultural traditions and customs. A key way of doing this is to observe important festivals during the course of the year. By subscribing to a variety of cultural practices, parents can also acquaint their children with Chinese history, customs, and folklore. Most of the celebrations are scheduled according to the lunar calendar, rather than the solar or Gregorian calendar used in the West. For this reason, many

Taiwanese keep calendars at home that have both the Western and lunar calendars. The lunar calendar dates are indicated in small Chinese characters alongside each Western calendar date. These bilingual calendars can be easily bought, but most families can obtain them free in December if they have been steady customers at a Chinese store, restaurant, or business.

In Taiwan there are many celebrations throughout the year. But in the United States, the ones that are commonly observed are somewhat fewer. Many of the festivals in Taiwan are associated with local temples or city gods, which are not present in the United States. Some of the most important festivals in the United States are the Chinese New Year, the Lantern Festival, the Dragon Boat Festival, and the Mid-Autumn Festival. Of these many observances, the Chinese New Year is the most widely celebrated. For other countries that use the lunar calendar, it is also their New Year. Thus, the Vietnamese know it as *Tet*, or the Vietnamese New Year.

Lunar New Year

The Lunar New Year is a joyous occasion for the Taiwanese community. Tied to the coming of spring, it is also known as *chunjie* or "spring festival." To make preparations for auspicious beginnings for the New Year, the house is cleaned ahead of time. No cleaning should be done during the first few days of the New Year, as that would sweep away the good luck. The Kitchen God is to return to the Jade Emperor to report on the status of the family. Supplications are made to the Kitchen God in hopes that he will deliver a favorable report, assuring good fortune for the coming year.

The house will be decorated with plants and flowers. Blooming peach and plum blossoms, water lilies, and narcissus flowers may be displayed to welcome the Lunar New Year. Fresh fruits such as oranges, tangerines, and pomegranates are placed in bowls. Trays of watermelon seeds, dried fruits, and candies wrapped in gold and red paper are put in trays. The family's container or bin where rice is stored is filled as a good omen for the New Year.

Red paper with beautiful calligraphy bearing good wishes will be put up on walls and by the doors. These spring couplets or *chunlian* will have expressions for prosperity, good luck, longevity, happiness, good health, peace, and other good wishes. Typical examples will be "Wishing You a Happy New Year," "Many Blessings and Long Life," "Good Health Throughout the Year," and "Success in All Your Undertakings." Merchants and storeowners will adorn their homes and businesses with those reading "Wishing You a Prosperous New Year," "May Your Business Ever Flourish," and "May the Fountain of Your Prosperity Continue to Grow." Characters for "spring (*chun*)" and "good fortune (*fu*)" will be placed upside down, because the sound for "upside down (*dao*)" is the same as that of "to come" or "to arrive."

Special foods are prepared before the New Year, many of which have symbolic meanings. In many cases, the foods have the same sounds as other words that mean good luck or good fortune. For example, vegetarian food (*zhai*) is cooked with different ingredients that are homonyms for the words signifying wealth, longevity, good luck, and many sons. Depending upon the household, items included can be mushrooms, dried bean curd, algae, fungi, moss, gingko nuts, and lotus seeds. A special pudding (*niangao*) made from glutinous rice flour is specially made for the New Year. Many kinds of rice cakes will also be made from sweet rice flour with taro, red beans, and large white radishes. Puffed rice cakes, a Hakka specialty, may be in evidence at this time of year.

Other foods prepared in advance of the New Year are dishes featuring chicken, pork, beef, fish, and lamb. Fish is especially welcome, for it is pronounced "*yu*," the same sound as the word for "surplus" or "abundance." The wish is that the family will not want for anything in the New Year. Meatballs, fishballs, steamed rice, and other foods are also readied. On New Year's Eve, they are arranged on a table before the family altar. As this is an occasion for family unity and harmony, everyone then gathers before the altar and pays their respects to the gods and ancestors. Incense may be lighted and wishes are extended for longevity for the parents and good fortune for the coming year. The family members then settle down to enjoy a sumptious repast. Children are encouraged to stay up all night and join in the socializing and rejoicing. In Taiwan, and in some communities in the United States such as Honolulu, families can set off firecrackers.

The New Year is a time to give gifts and have visits. During the New Year's celebrations, children may serve tea to their parents and elders. This act of courtesy demonstrates filial piety and respect for their parents and seniors. In turn, they will receive red envelopes (*hongbao*) containing "good luck" money. Relatives and friends visit those close to them and bring gifts. In exchange, they are offered tea and other refreshments. Older persons usually give the red envelopes to children that they know.

In general, this is a time for friendship and goodwill. Family members and friends do not exchange harsh words or quarrel. Mention of death, sickness, or other unfortunate events is avoided. Knives and sharp objects are put away so as to not cut off the string of good luck. Care is taken not to break dishes and bowls, as that would be a bad omen for the New Year. The New Year embodies the hope for a fresh start, and the hope is that everything that occurs in the first few days of the Lunar New Year will reflect that desire for a good beginning.

Lantern Festival

The Lantern Festival (*dengjie*), which occurs on the fifteenth day of the Lunar New Year, traditionally marks the end of the New Year's festivities. In Taiwan, the event is commemorated with festive lantern displays and parades. People show great creativity and imagination in creating colorful and breathtakingly beautiful lanterns. Traditionally, this is a time when a glutinous riceball soup called *yuanxiao* is served. The smooth round-shaped balls are a symbol of harmony and family togetherness. In the United States, lantern festivals have been observed in several communities in which there are large numbers of Chinese and Taiwanese residents.

In the United States, the Lunar New Year signals that many Chinese associations and Taiwanese organizations will start a round of spring banquets. It is a time to inaugurate the new officers and to celebrate the New Year. Organization leaders visit to pay their respects and to cement ties with other societies. There are banquets with many courses and cultural programs with music, performances, and speeches. But not all organizations hold their banquets at this time, for there are simply too many. Some will therefore schedule their events at a later date.

Dragon Boat Festival

The fifth day of the fifth lunar month is the occasion for the Upright Sun Festival (*duanyang jie*) or the Fifth Month Festival (*wuyue jie*). In China and Taiwan, summer began about this time. Summer with its heat and humidity might bring unpleasantness, disease, and bad health. Insects and pests multiplied in great abundance. People brought out charms, sachets, amulets, talismans, and herbs to ward off these illnesses and ailments.

The Fifth Month Festival also doubles as the Dragon Boat Festival (*longchuan jie*). During the Warring States period of the Zhou dynasty in China (403–221 B.C.), an upright and honest minister for the kingdom of Chu was maligned by his enemies and dismissed from his post. In protest against the corruption and wrongdoing of his opponents, Qu Yuan committed suicide by plunging into the Mi Lo River. His death is seen as an act of patriotism and courage, and the Chinese honor his memory by having colorful dragon boat races. The races are supposed to be attempts to rescue him and to recover his body. In Hong Kong and Taiwan, skilled teams paddle furiously to win the competitions. The exciting races are held before huge crowds and large numbers of tourists. With the drums beating and bright banners waving, the races put everyone into a festive mood. In the United States, the stirring dragon races have been introduced into a number of cities including Honolulu, San Francisco, Los Angeles, and Seattle.

A kind of special food called *zong* is also associated with the Dragon Boat Festival. According to tradition, it was thrown into the Mi Lo River as an offering to feed Qu Yuan's spirit. The food is a glutinous rice pudding wrapped in bamboo leaves and tied by string or thread. Inside the rice pudding are pork, beans, the yellow yolk of a duck's egg, and other ingredients. Other types of rice pudding can have other kinds of fillings such as vegetables. There are also rice puddings that are salty or sweet in flavor. The sweet *zong* can be dipped into sugar or syrup and then eaten. Because of the popularity of this food, it is prepared at other times as well. It can also be purchased in restaurants, supermarkets, and stores.

Mid-Autumn Festival

The Mid-Autumn Festival (*zhongqiu jie*) is also known as the Moon Festival. It falls on the fifteenth day of the eighth lunar month, a time when the full moon can be seen. People all around the world have stories about the moon, and the Chinese are no different. One account speaks of a woman Chang E who became the Moon Goddess after she swallowed a pill for immortality. The pill belonged to her husband, and she had taken it without his knowledge. Fearing his wrath, she fled, flew to the moon, and lives there still.

A very popular observance, the Mid-Autumn Festival is a time when families can just relax and admire the brightness of the round, full moon. Its smooth roundness is a symbol of family peace and harmony. In autumn's abundance, trays of fruit such as pomelos, pomegranates, plums, peaches, melons, grapes, and pears are placed on an altar as offerings for the moon goddess. There are also trays of delicious moon cakes, baked in the shape of the moon. All of this food can be eaten as the family gazes at the moon.

A wide assortment of moon cakes is available in all the Chinese bakeries at this time. The paste fillings can be made from lotus seeds, melon seeds, black beans, red beans, and mung beans. They can be plain or with yellow duck yolks. Whether the cake has one or two yolks determines its higher cost. Other moon cakes have nuts, coconut, sweetmeats, and other tasty fillings. Depending on the source, the crust or skin and texture of the cakes can be flaky, firm, or moist.

Stores and supermarkets selling Chinese groceries display moon cakes made in Taiwan, Hong Kong, China, and the United States in gaily colored tins or cardboard boxes. These containers hold four cakes, and people can purchase them for gifts. At the bakeries, different quantities can be bought. Because of the Chinese influence upon Vietnam, Vietnamese stores also sell moon cakes.

In a number of U.S. cities, community leaders have organized Mid-Autumn Festival celebrations. This is the case in Boston, San Francisco, Los Angeles, and elsewhere. A street fairlike atmosphere prevails, as booths sell moon cakes, Chinese pastries, foods, and drinks and display shirts, souvenirs, and books. Companies that want to promote themselves offer free samples or literature. Stages are set up where young school children dance, adults play musical instruments or sing songs and opera, and martial arts groups and lion dancers perform.

Other Observances

In addition to the festivals already mentioned, other events may be observed by the Taiwanese. One is the Clear and Bright Festival (*Qingming jie*), which is held in memory of ancestors. Held on the fifth day of the fourth lunar month, it is akin to Memorial Day. In Taiwan, families visit the cemeteries and grave sites to show respect for those who came before. The graves are swept clean, and food offerings are placed before them. For drinks there are cups of tea and wine. The food includes rice, cakes, buns, pork, fish, chicken, and other dishes. Chopsticks for the food, incense, candles, and paper money are also set down. After the rites are performed, the food can be shared and eaten.

Other important dates on the lunar calendar include the Double Seventh Festival, the Double Ninth Festival, and the Winter Solstice Festival. The Double Seventh Festival (*qiyueqi jie*) or Cowherd and Weaver-Maid Festival (*niulang zhinu jie*) is observed on the seventh day of the seventh lunar month. It celebrates the union of a cowherd and a weaver-maid who were separated except for this day. The cowherd was an ordinary mortal, while the weaver-maid was the youngest daughter of the Kitchen God. They had fallen in love and married, but the gods could not permit that union. Only once a year can they meet. The weaver-maid is seen as a protector of women and children, so offerings are made to her. The items include fruit, cosmetics, and vessels containing water.

The Double Ninth Festival (*Chongyang jie*) occurs on the ninth day of the ninth lunar month. It is an occasion to remember ancestors and to respect elders. It is an occasion to enjoy chrysanthemum wine, fly kites, and go hiking. The Winter Solstice Festival (*dongjie*) falls on the eleventh lunar month and usually takes place around December 22. It is the shortest day of the year and heralds the beginning of winter. Gods and ancestors are honored at the family altar and invited to participate in the celebration, which includes special offerings. Afterwards, the family can enjoy the foods that were prepared in advance.

In addition, there are observances tied to birthdays of key religious figures. An example is Guanyin, the Goddess of Mercy, whose birthday is celebrated on nineteenth day of the second lunar month. Another is Mazu, the Empress of Heaven, whose birthday comes on the twenty-third day of the third lunar month. Still another is the Buddha, specifically Gautama or Sakyamuni, whose birthday is observed on the eighth day of the fourth lunar month. These birthdays are joyfully celebrated at the temples that have been established throughout the United States.

Finally, the Ghost Month Festival (*guiyue*), celebrated on the fifteenth day of the seventh lunar month, is both a Buddhist and Daoist observance. The Buddhists refer to it as the Magnolia Festival (*yulanpen hui*). During this time, the souls of the dead are permitted to return briefly to earth. Buddhists priests will chant sutras and pray for the dead. They will also tell the filial story of Mulian (Maudgalyayana), Buddha's disciple, who accumulated merit to rescue his mother from hell. People offer food and beverages. They also burn incense, candles, and paper money to feed these hungry souls.

4

An Evolving Taiwanese American Identity

The Chinese can be found distributed throughout the world. Some scholars have even referred to a diaspora of Chinese who live outside China. In recent years, others have talked about a Greater China, which includes China, Taiwan, Hong Kong, and Macau. This Greater China is seen as a large economic and cultural bloc because of these countries' common ethnic background. There is a tendency by many in China to assume that these overseas Chinese are like them and will return to their roots. The Chinese have a saying, "Falling leaves return to the root (*luoye huigen*)." But Taiwanese Americans are not certain that they want Taiwan to be part of a Greater China, nor do they believe in the idea of returning to the Chinese root.

Among Taiwanese Americans today, an important issue is the matter of their identity. Are Taiwanese Americans distinct from Chinese Americans? Is Taiwanese culture different from Chinese culture? If so, is theirs any more different than that of the Cantonese or any of the regional cultures in China? This is a heated debate that is taking place in Taiwan, with some Taiwanese declaring that their culture is distinct. It is a debate that is being carried on among Taiwanese in the United States as well.

The question of Taiwanese identity is related to the international status of Taiwan. Is it to be an acceptance of the idea of one China with Taiwan having autonomy? Or is it to be independence for Taiwan with a separate Taiwan and a separate China? The Nationalist Party on Taiwan at the moment believes that there is one China but that the People's Republic of China does not represent it. International politics like domestic politics can be fluid, and situations can change. But it is a matter that affects Taiwanese identity.

FACTORS IN TAIWANESE IDENTITY

Several different factors have contributed to a sense of Taiwanese identity. One factor is the Taiwanese conflict with the mainlanders, especially after the February 28 Incident of 1947. Another factor is the role of the U.S. government and Taiwanese Americans. The desire for democracy and a more open political system has been nurtured to a significant degree by Taiwanese who were educated and had lived abroad. A third factor is the democratic change in the political system of Taiwan that makes it significantly different from China. A fourth factor is an interest in Taiwanese history and culture. And finally, the fifth factor is the political relationship with China.

Taiwanese Conflict with Mainlanders

One of the factors contributing to a Taiwanese identity is its conflict with the mainlanders. At the end of World War II, the Chinese government governed by the Nationalist Party took Taiwan back from Japan. The island had been lost during the Sino-Japanese War of 1894–95 and ceded under the terms of the Treaty of Shimonoseki of 1895. But as Chinese government officials and soldiers returned to Taiwan, tensions between the mainlanders and the Taiwanese mounted. Some mainlanders saw the Taiwanese as collaborators with the Japanese. The fifty years of Japanese rule had been a long separation. During this period, many Taiwanese learned to speak fluent Japanese. Moreover, they had adopted some Japanese customs and practices. When Japan needed soldiers for its war effort, Taiwanese were drafted to serve in the Japanese military during World War II.

On the other hand, Taiwanese saw the mainlanders as being arrogant and contemptuous towards them. When Taiwanese spoke their Minnan dialect of Fujianese, the mainlanders could not understand why they would not speak Mandarin Chinese and looked down upon them for their inability to speak this language fluently. Actually, under Japanese rule a strong system of colonial education from the elementary to the university level had been put in place. Although speaking Chinese was discouraged and learning Japanese was promoted, literacy had made great gains in Taiwan. At the same time, the Japanese authorities invested in building up the island's economic infrastructure by developing railroads, communications, and other public works. As a result, Taiwan was economically advanced in comparison with mainland China. The soldiers from the mainland were envious of the contrast between them and the Taiwanese.

As friction mounted, an unfortunate episode occurred on February 28,

1947. When a woman vendor was accosted and a person was killed, the pent up resentment of the native Taiwanese burst into the open. Angry riots flared up. The incident quickly spread, leading to civil unrest. A government crackdown followed with large numbers of Taiwanese being arrested and several thousand killed. The incident simmered in the memories of the native Taiwanese for years to come, but the government proscripted public mention of the affair. The February 28 Incident became Taiwan's secret history, known but not discussed.

On the mainland of China, a civil war continued to rage on. Once Japan had been defeated in 1945, the Chinese Nationalist government and the Chinese Communists no longer needed to maintain a semblance of unity against an external enemy. They openly fought against each other with massive numbers of troops. Despite American attempts at mediation, all efforts at compromise and finding peace failed. The Nationalists fared badly in their military campaigns and by 1949, they were forced to withdraw to Taiwan. The Communists marched into Beijing and on October 1, 1949, proclaimed the establishment of the People's Republic of China.

When the government of the Nationalists retreated to Taiwan, thousands of mainlanders followed them onto the island. A Republic of China on Taiwan with a complete national government was set up in the city of Taibei. Mainlanders commanded the government and bureaucratic posts, and the native Taiwanese were told to stay out of politics and tend to their daily work. In this fashion, there was a simple division of labor. Mandarin Chinese was taught in the schools and the speaking of Taiwanese in the schools was discouraged.

Martial law was imposed in 1949, as an attempt at a Communist takeover was expected. No dissent or criticism of the ruling Nationalist Party was permitted. The outbreak of the Korean War in 1950 led to U.S. participation in the civil war. President Harry Truman dispatched the Seventh Fleet and positioned it between Taiwan and the Chinese mainland, thereby preventing any Communist conquest of the island. In 1954, the United States and Taiwan signed a Mutual Defense Treaty in which Washington agreed to defend the island.

Because of U.S. policy intervening on behalf of Taiwan, two distinct political entities had emerged. One was the People's Republic of China with its capital in Beijing. The other was the Republic of China on Taiwan with its capital in Taibei. Some countries such as Great Britain recognized Beijing as the government of China. The United States, on the other hand, supported Taiwan and supplied it with foreign aid until 1965. It also provided military aid grants until 1974. Most important, it continued to recognize Taibei as the official government of China and maintained that the Republic of China should occupy the seat for China in the United Nations.

Meanwhile, during all this time since the end of World War II, the mainlander elite in the Nationalist Party dominated the politics of Taiwan. Under martial law and a sense of national emergency in a continuing civil war and rivalry with China, no dissent or criticism was permitted. Dissidents often had to remain abroad, in exile in Japan, the United States, or elsewhere. No other political parties were permitted to organize and challenge the dominance of the Nationalist Party. In essence, a transplanted group ruled the native Taiwanese population. This sense of unequal political power and unequal social status contributed to a sense of differences between the mainlanders and the Taiwanese population.

The Role of the United States and Taiwanese Americans

But the situation was beginning to change. By the 1970s, many governments around the world had recognized Beijing as the government of China. In 1971, the United Nations voted to admit China and to oust Taiwan. The United States was also moving to normalize relations with China. President Richard Nixon visited China the next year and with his national security adviser Henry Kissinger issued a Shanghai Communique. The document acknowledged that there was only one China and that Taiwan was a part of China. This paved the way for President Jimmy Carter to recognize Beijing as the official government of China in 1979. Formal diplomatic relations with Taiwan were broken off, and the U.S. Mutual Defense Treaty with the island was ended.

After thirty years of supporting Taibei, the United States had finally recognized Beijing as the official government of China. For Taiwan, the turnabout was painful. It had always claimed to represent all of China and had been long been successful in keeping Beijing out of the United Nations and other world organizations. Now the shoe was on the other foot. Its diplomatic relations with other nations and organizations steadily eroded. In the Olympic games of 1984, Taiwan could only compete as "Chinese Taibei." It could not claim to be the Republic of China or China. The scenario was repeated in the Asian Games and other international organizations such as the Asia-Pacific Economic Cooperation forum (APEC) and the Asian Development Bank (ADB).

The United States, its former ally, maintained a lower profile in Taiwan. While it no longer formally recognized Taibei was the government of China,

Washington knew that it still had important economic and political ties to Taiwan. The Taiwan Relations Act of 1979 allowed the United States to maintain the American Institute in Taiwan to watch over its interests. Taiwan was permitted to open the Coordination Council of North American Affairs in the United States with the same role. In essence, the two organizations served the functions of embassies but at an informal level. Taiwan later changed its name from the Coordination Council of North American Affairs to the Taibei Economic and Cultural Representative Office.

From 1949 onward, the United States had played an important role in determining Taiwan's fate. Had it not stationed its Seventh Fleet in the Taiwan Strait in 1950, signed a Mutual Defense Treaty in 1954, and furnished foreign and military aid, Taiwan might not have existed as a separate country. U.S. policy has been crucial in assuring Taiwan's independence, which is one reason why a strong Republic of China lobby has attempted to influence Congress, the White House, and the American public (Bachrack 1976; Newman 1983; Koen 1974).

But who was influencing whom? It was a two-way street. Despite its recognition of Beijing in 1979, the United States continued to have considerable leverage in Taiwan. In the 1970s, it applied pressure on Taiwan's Nationalist government to liberalize its policies towards the native Taiwanese. It urged that Taibei show greater openness and tolerance for opposing political viewpoints and parties. The Nationalist government could not disregard American concern, as Taiwan's existence as an independent state continued to depend on U.S. involvement on its behalf.

That the American government pressed for changes in the internal politics of Taiwan was partly due to the mobilization by Taiwanese in the United States. This included both native Taiwanese and mainlander critics of the Nationalist government. Many of these Taiwanese had originally come to the United States as students and had remained as professionals and intellectuals. But having been exposed to American ideas regarding a free press and democratic politics, many yearned to have a similar situation in Taiwan. Many were particularly upset to learn about the Gaoxiong incident in 1979. At a demonstration for human rights in the city of Gaoxiong in Taiwan, there had been a government crackdown with many arrested. Eventually a number of those apprehended were to receive jail sentences for sedition. In addition, some Taiwanese were also interested in learning more about mainland China, a subject that was considered politically sensitive on Taiwan.

Several different factors helped to galvanize the Taiwanese dissidents and critics in the United States. The Nationalist government was accused of monitoring its students who had been studying abroad. In the 1970s, there were many allegations at major universities in the United States that this was the case. Campus newspapers ran articles on how it was done, mentioning that older graduate students seemed to be spying on their peers. In some cases, school newspapers even reproduced the forms that were purportedly used in the files on the Taiwanese students. These charges continued into the 1980s (*Los Angeles Times* 7/31/81:23; *San Francisco Chronicle* 10/8/82; Tucker 1994:152–53; Cohen 1988:294–95).

Repercussions could follow from these reports. In 1968, a graduate student in economics at the University of Hawaii was deported to Taiwan from Japan. Chen Yuxi (Chen Yu-hsi) then was arrested for having read newspapers and literature from mainland China. This was considered subversive activity and potentially dangerous. He received a sentence of seven years in prison (Kaplan 1992:149). In 1981, a Taiwanese American professor who was visiting Taibei mysteriously fell to his death. Chen Wencheng (Chen Wen-chen), a professor at Carnegie-Mellon University in Pittsburgh, had been a member of a Taiwan democratic opposition group. After he arrived in Taiwan, he was seized by authorities for questioning. Later, his body was found behind the library of National Taiwan University. The government reported that he had either committed suicide or had accidentally fallen to his death. But his wife and others claimed that he had been murdered (Tenorio 1981:IV-3, 6; Park 1981:2–4; Chai 1981:8–9). Later, a Professor Chen Wen-Chen Memorial Foundation was established in 1982 to offer scholarships for deserving students (*Taiwan Tribune* 3/8/97:8).

The death of journalist Henry Liu in California brought even greater notoriety. In 1984, using the pen name "Jiang Nan," Liu had written a critical biography of Jiang Jingguo, the president of the Republic of China. Shortly thereafter, he was assassinated in his Daly City home near San Francisco. The death triggered an investigation that suggested involvement by high intelligence and government officials in Taiwan. Concerned members of Congress held hearings that exposed numerous instances of harassment of Taiwanese in the United States. The whole episode raised a storm of unfavorable publicity about the Nationalist government (Kaplan 1992; Berman 1992:126–27).

Nonetheless, as the Taiwanese community and students in the United States grew, more debates and discussions about Taiwan occurred. In the more open climate of the United States, many Taiwanese groups and organizations were formed, some of which explored the possibilities for political reform and self-determination. They included the World United Formosans for Independence (WUFI) started in 1970 and the Formosan Christians for Self-Determination in 1972. Others included the Formosan Association for

Human Rights (FAHR) in 1976 and the Formosan Association for Public Affairs (FAPA) in 1982. The Formosan Club of America, made up of many clubs in the 1960s and 1970s, became the Taiwanese Association of America (TAA). Many of these organizations maintained ties with other Taiwanese groups in Japan, Canada, Australia, and Europe. There were also publications, newsletters, and bulletins, such as the *Taiwan Communique* started in 1980 and the *Taiwanese Collegian* in 1983.

An important figure in the Taiwanese dissident community was Peng Mingmin. A professor and chair of the political science department at National Taiwan University, he had advocated a democratic and independent Taiwan. For taking this stance, he was arrested and sentenced to prison in 1964. When he was released, he went to the United States and continued to make his case by lecturing at universities and before community groups. Other activists and reformers of similar sentiments stayed in the United States and communicated their views to the American press, Congress, and the public. This led to Congressional hearings and media coverage which damaged the Nationalist government's image in the United States.

Political Liberalization in Taiwan

Jiang Jieshi's death in 1975 allowed his son Jiang Jingguo to succeed him as president. The younger Jiang found himself tested on several fronts. First of all, in the international arena, the Republic of China found its position severely compromised. Since 1971, many countries and international organizations had decided to recognize the People's Republic of China. Taiwan was increasingly isolated and alone. Second, in 1979, even the United States had recognized China and broken off formal diplomatic relations with Taiwan. This was particularly ominous, for it could be argued that the United States had been responsible for Taiwan's independence since 1949. In the face of these developments, Jiang Jingguo was aware that Taiwan could ill afford to be seen as a pariah nation that mistreated its people. That would compromise its political legitimacy and give further advantage to Beijing in its quest to be the government of a unified China.

Finally, political activists and dissidents within Taiwan repeatedly challenged the ruling Nationalist Party. It was illegal to organize an opposition political party, but they wanted reforms that would permit a more democratic system of government. To this end, they formed a coalition of politicians that were outside the ruling Nationalist Party. For this reason, they were labeled politicians that were *dangwai* or "outside the party." Although they faced arrest and harassment, they registered gains in elections to the Taiwan provincial assembly. These victories indicated that a growing segment of the population favored liberalization of the political system and sympathized with their efforts.

Cognizant of the changes in public sentiment, Jiang opened the door for political reforms. He implemented steps to permit the organization of political parties. He paved the way for elections to the representative bodies at the national, provincial, and local levels. In 1987, martial law was terminated. He also saw a need to bring more native Taiwanese into the Nationalist Party so that it could be more representative of the general population. Whether he had been farsighted, or whether he had been forced into adopting these changes, or whether it was a little bit of both, these moves had important consequences in making politics in Taiwan much more democratic.

When Jiang died in 1988, his successor Li Denghui introduced further reforms in Taiwan. Li himself was a native Taiwanese who had been educated in Japan and the United States. In fact, he had received his Ph.D. in agricultural economics from Cornell University in 1968. Li continued to promote Taiwanese participation in the Nationalist Party. Moreover, he made key appointments that elevated more Taiwanese to high government posts. After a government study of the February 28 Incident of 1947, Li formally apologized for the episode in 1995. Finally, he opened the office of president to direct election by the public. The presidential election of 1996 was widely seen as as a major step in the democratization of Taiwan. In this contest, Li won reelection to the presidency.

The overall effect of the changes instituted by Jiang Jingguo and Li Denghui was dramatic. It opened the way for multiparty political competition. Taiwan was no longer a state with a single party. In addition to the Nationalists, there were other competing parties. One was the Democratic Progressive Party (*Minzhu jinbudang*), made up predominantly of Taiwanese with Peng Mingmin as its leader. He had been able to return to Taiwan because of the liberalized political climate and in 1996 had even run unsuccessfully for president against Li Denghui. Another party was the New Party (*Xindang*), which was composed mostly of mainlanders. Because of the election reforms, Taiwan presented a clear contrast to the political system in China. This makes Taiwanese less than eager to be united with China.

The Taiwan Difference

While Taiwan was relegated to a peripheral and marginalized status in the international arena, its economic power became ever more formidable. By the 1980s, Taiwan had turned into an economic miracle. It was touted as one of the dynamos of Asia and mentioned with Japan, Hong Kong, Singapore, and South Korea. Background factors for this transformation were the Japanese colonial policies in Taiwan during the occupation period, U.S. foreign aid and technical assistance, land reform in Taiwan, a successful policy of economic development, and a favorable world climate. As a result, even as Taiwan was shunned diplomatically, businessmen and foreign governments all rushed to develop stronger economic ties and relationships with the island.

As these economic changes took place, Taiwanese participated in the improved business climate and prosperity. The numbers of professionals, intellectuals, scholars, and those in the middle class expanded noticeably. In the midst of growing affluence and rapid change, a nostalgia for the past developed. People became increasingly interested in the regional history of Taiwan, distinct from that of China. Along with this, there was a fascination with the folk culture, religion, art, dance, opera, and architecture of Taiwan. Literature played a key role as a group of writers from the 1970s onward were identified with a local, nativist perspective (*xiangtu wenxue*). Besides writing about a life that was vanishing and the conflicts accompanying modernization, authors were using local dialects and local idioms. As Taiwan's political system opened up, candidates running for political office vied with one another in speaking Taiwanese. A renewed interest in learning and speaking Taiwanese and Hakka became fashionable.

At the same time, Western influences were merging with traditional culture to form new syntheses. With the expansion of the educated middle class, Taiwan developed a flourishing audience for the arts and culture. Given the desire for creativity in the arts and culture, it is not surprising that artists, dancers, musicians, film producers, and others should be pioneering into new directions. There was syncretism and experimentation as groups such as the Cloud Gate Dance Ensemble (Yunmen) explored new forms. Lin Hwaimin, who founded the ensemble, had studied modern dance with the Martha Graham School in New York. He has since returned to try to develop a dance that can draw from Taiwan's past even as it also borrows from the West. The sizeable middle class has meant more consumers to support a dynamic community of Taiwanese artists and performers.

Relations with China

Part of the reason for Taiwan's quest for a separate identity is its determination to remain apart from China. With the liberalization that has taken place in recent years, its political system is a decided contrast to that of China.

Taiwan is much more open, tolerant, and democratic. It permits multiparty competition and dissenting points of view in the press and public. As a result, many of the people in Taiwan have no desire to be united with a country that they feel is behind not only in terms of freedom and self-expression but also in economic development.

Taiwan's attitudes to China have oscillated through time. For example, during the 1980s, relations between Taiwan and China were relaxed so that people could visit the Chinese mainland. Many Taiwanese visited Fujian, the province that had been the source of many immigrants to the island in the past. So many visited that it seemed that there was a "China fever" in vogue. Newspapers even had stories about Taiwanese marrying women from China. For a while, too, "Descendants of the Dragon," a song by Chang Mingmin, was extremely popular. The song proclaimed a pride in being Chinese and extolled the grandeur of the Chinese past. The Taiwanese songwriter even left Taiwan to live in China for awhile.

But several key episodes have instilled a fear of China in Taiwan. Under Deng Xiaoping, it appeared that China was gradually heading towards a more open political system. The pragmatic Deng had created a more hospitable climate for capitalism in China. It seemed that it was also moving towards a greater tolerance for dissent and differing political opinions. But on June 4, 1989, the forceful Communist suppression of demonstrators at Tiananmen Square in Beijing shocked the world. Captured on television cameras for all the world to see, the Tiananmen Incident triggered grave concern among the people of Taiwan. For the residents of Hong Kong, who were destined to be united with China in 1997, the event aroused anger, sadness, and widespread protest demonstrations.

Another episode was the presidential election in March 1996. Both Beijing and Taibei had long maintained that there was only one China, with Taiwan being a part of it. Beijing became suspicious about Li Denghui, because he was a native Taiwanese who was opening the presidency to direct elections in 1996. It saw direct elections for president as being the prelude to eventual independence for Taiwan as a separate nation. As a result, China conducted military exercises off Taiwan. They even fired missiles into the waters off Taiwan. To demonstrate its concern, the United States deployed two aircraft carrier battle groups close to Taiwan.

Even before the presidential elections, other actions by Taiwan had raised anxiety in Beijing. Just prior to the presidential election, Li Denghui had gone to the United States in 1995 to receive an honorary degree from Cornell University. Beijing saw the move as a bid to raise the stature of Taiwan as an independent nation, apart from China. Moreover, Taiwan had for some time been aggressively campaigning to gain admittance into international organizations such as the United Nations and the World Bank. But the Chinese attempts at intimidation in 1996 only firmed up the resolve on Taiwan to go through with the presidential elections and the reelection of Li. Nonetheless, the signal seemed to be that China was willing to use force against Taiwan. The Taiwanese were wary about an aggressive, dominant China. As a result, some say that the Taiwanese are culturally Chinese, but politically Taiwanese.

And yet, China and Taiwan are inextricably and increasingly bound together in complex ways. First of all, China sees Taiwan as a source of capital, expertise, and technology. Taiwan views China as a site for investment, labor, and other economic opportunities. The two entities have become intertwined economically, selling exports to each other and buying imports as well. Second, with Hong Kong's return to China in 1997, to be followed by Macau two years later, Taiwan's ties to China are becoming even more extensive. Hong Kong is a large market and a major hub in Asia for international capital, tourism, transportation, and communication. In the past, Hong Kong has received a large quantity of exports from Taiwan and has allowed it economic access to the Chinese mainland. For this reason, Taiwan wishes to maintain its ties with the former British colony. Taibei hopes that Beijing will adhere to its pledge of "one country, two systems" for Hong Kong. Finally, the people in Taiwan are also interested in the cultural heritage of China, while the people in China are fascinated by the cultural trends and fashions in Taiwan.

THE CONSTRUCTION OF TAIWANESE AMERICAN IDENTITY

In the United States, immigrants from Taiwan have also dealt with the question of Taiwanese identity. In organizations, publications such as the *Taiwan Tribune*, and even on the Internet, there have been attempts to develop a case for a Taiwanese identity apart from that of China. This could then bolster the claim that Taiwan deserves to exist as a separate country. An important aspect of this rationale for a distinctive identity rests on an interpretation of Taiwan's history and culture as being different. In this regard, some Taiwanese American publications such as the *Formosan Quarterly*, the *Taiwanese Collegian*, and *Taiwan Culture* had covers with folk art style depictions of Taiwanese farmers, aborigines, water buffalos, temples, and so forth to remind people of Taiwan's past.

History, Identity, and Transnational Politics

In some Taiwanese interpretations of their history, the Chinese have not cared about the people who lived on the island.[1] Ignored if not misruled by Chinese officials, according to these views, the residents of Taiwan adapted to a new frontier and created a distinctive Taiwan culture. As a Taiwanese folk saying put it, "There are Chinese fathers, but no Chinese mothers (*you tangren gong, wu tangren ma*)." This refers to the fact that male migrants intermarried with aborigines to form their own hybrid society. The Taiwanese may have partially originated from the Chinese, but they evolved their own history and developed their own society. Much later, China's willingness to cede Taiwan to Japan in 1895, after the defeat in the Sino-Japanese War, amounted to a betrayal of its residents. This again showed the insensitivity and disregard China had for the feelings of the Taiwanese.

After World War II, Taiwan was dominated by the influx of mainlanders from China. Taiwanese self-determination was stymied by the Nationalist government on Taiwan which claimed that it ruled for all of China. Taiwanese self-expression was also suppressed and denied respectability. Only after the legitimacy of the Nationalist government had been eroded in the global arena were there attempts at liberalization and reform in politics. But it was also because there had been repeated efforts at change by Taiwanese, some of whom had to contend with persecution and imprisonment. In short, past experience has demonstrated that rule by China and the mainlanders has hardly benefited the Taiwanese.

In writings espousing a Taiwanese American identity, there is often a "we" versus "they" division. The "we" are the Taiwanese, who include the aborigines, the Fujianese, and the Hakka. The "they" are the mainlanders. If the mainlanders would accept Taiwan as their homeland and learn the Taiwanese dialect, then they could also become Taiwanese. The groups that comprise the "we" are assumed to be united, but that is hardly the case. In recent years, the aborigines have sought greater recognition for their own identity. They have pushed for an end to being referred to as "compatriots living in mountains (*shanbao*)," for they also lived on the western plain of Taiwan. This campaign has finally won acceptance from the Nationalist government (Yun 1997:4–11; *Free China Journal* 5/22/92:2).

In fact, the Taiwanese Americans in Honolulu recognize a parallel between the Hawaiian sovereignty movement and the aborigines on Taiwan. Much as Americans seized the Hawaiian islands from the natives in 1893, the Han (and this includes Fujianese and Hakka) played a role in appropriating land from the aborigines. The aborigines do not consider Taiwan a frontier as they already lived there. As a result, the Taiwan aborigines have parallels to the experience of American Indians and native Hawaiians ("Hawaiian History" 1995:1–2).

The Hakka have historically had conflict with the Fujianese in Taiwan, too. These tensions can be compared to the conflicts between the Hakka and the Guangdong local residents (*bendiren*) in Southeastern China. The friction was over competition for land, water, and resources. Stereotyping over different dialects used and contrasting customs exacerbated the situation. Although relations between the Hakka and the Fujianese have somewhat improved, some Hakka thought of starting a separate political party in Taiwan several years ago. As Taiwan continues to evolve politically, Fujianese relations with the aborigines, the Hakka, and the mainlanders may also change.

Because of the large population of Taiwanese in the United States, there is a network that can help to maintain this sense of a distinct Taiwanese American identity. From the many organizations to the printed and electronic media, Taiwanese Americans can be sustained in their awareness of the "Taiwanese difference." Social functions, meetings, and forums provide opportunities to hear the Taiwanese folk songs, opera, and dialect. Visitors coming from Taiwan also strengthen a sense of Taiwanese identity.

Taiwanese Americans are certainly concerned about the fate of Taiwan. In the 1996 presidential election, some returned to vote for their candidates. Taibei had determined that overseas Taiwanese could participate in the presidential election. Chinese newspapers in the United States were filled with advertisements and stories about support groups in different cities campaigning for the different parties in Taiwan. The Taiwanese community was abuzz with discussion about who would win, what would be the consequences, and how China would react.

The Second Generation

But while the sense of a Taiwanese identity may be held by first-generation Taiwanese Americans, that may not be the case for the second generation. Second-generation Taiwanese Americans, born in the United States, have not had the same experiences as their parents. For them, Taiwan is a distant place, a place talked about by their fathers and mothers and studied in geography books. If ethnic identity is a community of memories, they do not share the same memories and perspectives as their parents. This is perhaps illustrated by the contrasts in reactions in the Little League World Series championships and the Olympic games. Taiwan has had a fantastic record in international competition in baseball, winning seventeen world championships by 1996. The Taiwanese parents routinely cheer for Taiwan to win in baseball, but to their consternation, their children cheer for the United States.

When the second-generation Taiwanese Americans visit Taiwan, they realize that they feel more comfortable in the United States. They find that in the United States they are seen as Asians instead of Americans. But when they are in Taiwan, they are regarded as Americans instead of Asians. They are not comfortable or fluent in speaking Taiwanese or Mandarin Chinese, and many cannot read the Chinese characters. They even feel discomfited and embarrassed when their parents and their friends unconsciously and spontaneously speak Taiwanese in the presence of others who only understand the English language.

Given this situation, some of the first generation feel an urgent imperative in trying to instill a sense of Taiwanese identity in their children. This concern is not unlike that felt by most immigrant parents who worry about their offspring in America. They fear a diluting of the cultural inheritance. As a result, there are active attempts to kindle an awareness of Taiwanese identity in the second generation.

Parents try to get their children to go to a Taiwanese church, language school, or summer camp with other Taiwanese. They try to socialize frequently with other Taiwanese so that the children can meet others of their own age. Moreover, they make occasional trips to Taiwan to acquaint their children with the birthplace of their parents. Alternatively, their children are enrolled in the summer youth language programs sponsored each year by the Republic of China.

There are also specific attempts to educate the second generation in Taiwanese history and culture. An example would be the Second Generation Network recently initiated by the Formosan Association for Political Affairs. First-generation Taiwanese American activists see a need to acquaint the second generation with the rationale for a Taiwanese identity, lamenting, as do other first-generation immigrant groups, the acculturation and disinterest in cultural identity among their offspring. The Second Generation Network is an attempt to reach out to the second generation who are primarily English-speaking and to involve them in leadership training and lobbying activities with Congress (E. Chen 1997).

The Second Generation Network is interesting because it openly recognizes the language difference that is occurring with the younger generation of Taiwanese Americans. It acknowledges that the second generation is going to be more fluent in English. At the same time, it realizes that Taiwanese

American organizations require fresh, new membership to sustain them. The situation is not unlike the Japanese American Citizens League, a second-generation *nisei* organization that is trying to recruit third generation *sansei* Japanese Americans to take over its functions. The difficult question for many ethnic groups is whether it will be possible to interest a younger generation in entering an organization that primarily caters to the views and agendas of a previous generation.

For many ethnic groups language is seen as a marker of identity. Although the Second Generation Network has another view on the matter, many Taiwanese Americans are concerned that the second generation is unable to speak Taiwanese fluently. This is also the situation in contemporary Taiwan. Many of the youth born in the last two decades can speak Mandarin Chinese more fluently than the Taiwanese of their parents. This is partly because Mandarin Chinese is the language of instruction in the schools in Taiwan. As a a result, there are now active attempts by first-generation Taiwanese Americans to teach the youth how to speak, read, and write Taiwanese. Instruction in Taiwanese is available on several Internet sites. Some also use the Bible translated into Taiwanese by the Taiwanese Presbyterian Church for this purpose.

A problem in the teaching of Taiwanese, however, is that many characters do not exist for the words. As a result, different romanizations using the English alphabet are being developed to substitute for the words that have no characters. A concern is how to systematize this, as the Fujian dialects are also spoken in the mainland province, in Southeast Asia, and among the growing numbers of Fujianese Americans in the United States. Some Taiwanese linguists have authored language texts that can teach history and culture as well. Publications such as the *Taiwen Tongxun* (*Tai-bun Thong-Sin* or *Taiwanese Writing Forum*) and the *Taiwan Baihe Luntan* (*Taiwanese Lily Forum*) try to promote the use of the Taiwanese language. Several universities such as the University of Hawaii, the University of California at Berkeley, and Cornell University have recently offered instruction on Taiwanese. But like Cantonese, it is not widely taught. The Hakka have also attempted to encourage an interest in their history and language.

Particularly noteworthy is the publication of Taiwanese cookbooks in English. One example is that of the Northern California chapter of the North American Taiwanese Women's Association. It recently issued a cookbook with the title *Taiwanese Homestyle Cooking* (1995). That such cookbooks are being made available in any immigrant community or ethnic group indicates the presence of a growing second generation that does not know how to prepare its homeland's homestyle cooking. In addition to these recipes, the

Northern California group's cookbook includes cultural explanations about the backgrounds for various festivals and celebrations.

Intergroup Relations

Although some Taiwanese consider Taiwanese culture different from Chinese culture, in the United States identity for Taiwanese Americans is actually very fluid. It is as if they have multi-layered identities, whereby they can be Taiwanese American, Chinese American, Asian American, and American. It depends on the situation, the community, and the individuals involved. In this respect, they may not be unlike Cantonese in the United States who are different from those who speak Mandarin Chinese. Depending on the occasion, the Cantonese may interact solely with other Cantonese. But at another event, they may join together with other Mandarin-speaking Chinese, Asian Americans, or other Americans.

Taiwanese Americans live in the United States with Chinese Americans. These Chinese Americans have backgrounds that are far from uniform. The first-generation immigrants are from Hong Kong, Macau, Singapore, Southeast Asia, and China. Of those from Southeast Asia, many are Chinese from Vietnam, Laos, Cambodia, Thailand, Malaysia, and the Philippines. The Chinese from China are from Guangdong, Fujian, and elsewhere. As a result, the dialects that can be heard among the Chinese who are not from Taiwan can include Cantonese, Hakka, Chaozhou, Fujian, and Mandarin Chinese. The Cantonese from the Longdu areas of Guangdong actually speak a dialect of Fujianese.

The many differences among Chinese Americans is well illustrated in film producer Wayne Wang's movie *Chan is Missing* (1981). In the plot, a person by the name of Chan is missing. But in trying to find him, the film makes fun of all the stereotypes about Chinese. There are Chinese from all walks of life and all kinds of backgrounds. A Taiwanese cook drinks milk to soothe his stomach. Another character says that apple pies from Chinatown are Chinese because of the difference in the pie crust. In short, it notes that Chinese Americans are a complex and variegated community (Wang 1994).

The majority of the Chinese population in the United States is foreign born. As a result, the second generation of Chinese Americans have much in common with second-generation Taiwanese Americans. In playwright David Henry Hwang's play *FOB*, there is conflict between an ABC and the FOB. "ABC" refers to American-born Chinese, while "FOB" alludes to Fresh-Off-the-Boat or those who have recently arrived (Hwang 1990). As with other immigrant groups culture clashes occur between those who are more acculturated and those who are not. In Hwang's play, one of the new immigrants keeps asking for *congyoubing*. This is a scallion cake, which is a favorite with many including those from Taiwan.

Even though the first-generation Taiwanese are trying to teach the second generation to be more fluent in the Taiwanese language and to read Chinese characters, that may be an uphill struggle. The second generation are more likely to read Asian American literature and other works in English. If they subscribe to papers and magazines, they are more disposed to get those printed in English, such as *Transpacific, A. Magazine, Yolk, Face,* and *Asianweek.* The first four are glossy magazines with slick color and a materialistic "yuppie" orientation for young professionals. They deal with entertainment, stars, newsmakers, and noteworthy events. In short, they seek to appeal to a younger generation that is interested in being trendy and fashionable. The pages in these publications present a cosmopolitan, chic look for a relatively affluent Asian American middle class. The advertisers are on the upscale side in terms of cosmetics, clothing, cars, wine, investment companies, travel companies, cellular phones, computers, and so forth. Madison Avenue, it seems, has discovered the Asian American market.

Taiwanese Americans interact with Chinese Americans at many different levels. When they look at the headlines, they are aware of television figures such the former CBS-TV anchor Connie Chung and master chef Martin Yan. They know about architects such as Maya Ying Lin, who designed the Vietnam Veterans Memorial in Washington, D.C., and also I. M. Pei, who designed the East Wing of the National Gallery of Art in Washington, D.C., and the expansion of the Louvre in Paris. They can see on television athletes such as tennis star Michael Chang, Olympic gymnast Amy Chow, and figure-skating champion Michelle Kwan. They can see or hear the musical performances by Yo-Yo Ma and the films by producers such as Wayne Wang and Arthur Dong. They can read the works by authors such as Maxine Hong Kingston, Amy Tan, and Lawrence Yep. Finally, they are aware of Chinese Americans who have received national recognition in politics. One was Hiram Fong from Hawaii, the first Chinese American and first Asian American to have served in the U.S. Senate. Another was Gary Locke of Washington, the first Chinese American to have become the governor of a state.

When there are Chinese American events and celebrations, they may participate separately or jointly. This can include community observances of the Chinese New Year and the Lunar New Year, Mid-Autumn Festivals, and Dragon Boat races. When competitions for Miss Chinatown U.S.A. or local areas take place, they also participate. In fact, in a number of instances, Taiwanese Americans have won their contests and even won at the national level. Included among the prizes was a free trip to Taiwan, Hong Kong, and China.

In politics, Taiwanese Americans are aware of the need to work with Chinese Americans. They may join in common cause with the Chinese American Citizens Alliance (CACA) or the Organization of Chinese Americans (OCA). Both of these organizations are active in behalf of Chinese American issues, and the Organization of Chinese Americans maintains an office in the nation's capital to monitor issues that may affect Chinese Americans. The Taiwanese American Citizens League has on several occasions cooperated with these Chinese American organizations. There are also Taiwanese who have joined these groups, most especially the Organization of Chinese Americans, which has many chapters throughout the United States.

Taiwanese Americans realize that they will be often be identified as Chinese Americans or Asian Americans. To the extent that there are instances of discrimination that affect any Asians in the United States, they may have consequences for Taiwanese Americans as well. As a result, Taiwanese Americans are very concerned about the representations of Asian Americans before the media and the American public. In the late 1970s and early 1980s, the U.S. automobile industry faced severe competition from Japan. During this period, the resentment of rivalry from Japan was expressed in Japan-bashing. Unfortunately, as a result of this anger and stereotyping, a Chinese by the name of Vincent Chin was killed in Detroit in 1982. On the day before his wedding, he was clubbed to death by two unemployed workers using baseball bats who blamed him for the loss of their jobs.

Knowing that Asian Americans may face prejudice and discrimination in the United States, Taiwanese Americans have joined many Asian American organizations. A look at the membership of these organizations shows Taiwanese participation in Asian American Law Caucuses in several different cities. The law caucuses provide assistance to individuals on issues that affect the Asian American community. The Taiwanese are also active in groups such as the Asian American Journalists Association that try to present more informed views about the different Asians in the United States.

Taiwanese Americans who attend universities are often students in Asian American Studies classes. They learn about the history of Asians in the United States, including the Chinese, Japanese, Koreans, Filipinos, Asian Indians, and Southeast Asians. They hear about the difficulties faced by the early immigrants in adapting to a new environment and contending with racism and discrimination. They are aware that Angel Island in San Francisco Bay was the Ellis Island of the West. Chinese and other Asians who came to the West Coast were often detained there. They become acquainted with the legacy of anti-Asian laws and immigration policies that restricted or ended the flow of Asians to the United States until the period of World War II and after. Previous struggles by Asians have made Taiwanese immigration into the United States possible.

Since the 1960s, many Taiwanese Americans have joined in promoting cultural diversity and multiculturalism in the United States. They support the idea of a national Asian Pacific American Heritage Month. They join in cultural groups such as the East/West Players of Los Angeles, the Asian American Theater Company of San Francisco, and the Pan Asian Repertory Theater of New York. They support other activities that can help to promote tolerance and understanding of Asians in the United States as well. These include Chinese American historical societies, museums, and exhibits, Asian American film festivals, and educational efforts. This effort also involves joining in multiethnic coalitions on issues of common concern with groups other than Asian Americans. It may touch upon matters of pertaining to discrimination and prejudice, community, education, health care, immigration, public safety, and other social issues.

THE TAIWANESE AMERICAN LEGACY

Despite the relatively short history of the Taiwanese in United States, they have been a significant presence. Most came after the immigration changes in 1965, but they have already helped to alter the U.S. cultural landscape. They have joined in the reinventing of America, much like the successive waves of immigrants that came before them. But instead of being FOB or "Fresh Off the Boat," the Taiwanese Americans have come as FOP or "Fresh Off the Plane." Since their arrival, the Taiwanese have rendered important contributions in many different ways.

First, with world attention focused on Asia and the Pacific Rim, Taiwanese Americans are well poised to help the United States compete in the global economy. Because many are first-generation immigrants and have experience in Asia, they are well equipped to be cultural brokers in penetrating the markets of Asia. They know how to arrange deals and to be sensitive to the cultural practices of the different countries. Highly educated and bilingual, they can also link up with Chinese entrepreneurs in Taiwan, Hong Kong, China, Singapore, and Southeast Asia.

The Taiwanese have in addition brought capital and investment into the United States. Particularly on the West Coast, Taiwanese banks have been started up. Alert to business opportunities, Taiwanese capitalists have started enterprises and built office, shopping, and housing complexes. Willing to

The grand opening of a business at a shopping mall. Courtesy of Polly Lo.

take a chance, they have provided the start-up funds for many new ventures that have helped to provide business opportunities and employment. In this sense, they have assisted in improving the economic climate in the regions in which they reside. An example of a successful entrepreneur is Jerry Yang of Yahoo!, an Internet navigational guide company. Another example is John Tu and David Sun of Kingston Technology Corporation, a Silicon Valley business.

The first-generation Taiwanese are immigrants, but according to economists, they are also a form of human capital. They are a brain drain of talent and expertise from Taiwan in the form of professionals, scholars, scientists, computer specialists, engineers, and businessmen. Taiwan has assumed the costs in preparing and educating them, but the United States has been the beneficiary as the receiving country. In the universities, corporations, laboratories, and workplaces in America, the Taiwanese have helped to upgrade U.S. science and research.

Firms in Silicon Valley or industrial parks, as well as noted corporations like IBM, have large pools of Taiwanese talent. From the achievements of Dr. David Ho in AIDS research to Professor Paul Chu in superconductivity experiments, the Taiwanese have helped keep America on the cutting edge of science and technology. Astronauts like Edward Lu are extending the frontiers of science into space as well. That Dr. Chang-lin Tien should have served as the president of the University of California at Berkeley was par-

A restaurant offers Taiwanese food, soybean milk, and baked goods. Courtesy of Polly Lo.

ticularly apt, for it was symbolic of the vital roles played in American universities by Taiwanese American faculty.

Because of their family values emphasizing education, younger and second-generation Taiwanese Americans have excelled in their academic studies. Each year, the Westinghouse Science Talent Search Competition places the spotlight on those who are America's hope for the future in science and technology. Invariably a number of Taiwanese Americans are among the finalists. Their number might include future Nobel Prize winners like Yuan-tse Lee, formerly on the faculty of the University of California at Berkeley. Other Taiwanese youth excel in scholarship and win admission to prestigious universities all across the United States.

Beyond their accomplishments in business, science, and education, Taiwanese Americans have made important contributions to cultural life in the United States. Taiwanese artists, musical groups, and musicians have shared their talent with American audiences in museums, concert halls, theaters, and arenas. One example is renowned violinist Cho-liang Lin on the faculty of the Juilliard School. Another of the most prominent of the Taiwanese artists is Ang Lee, the film director. His films such as *Pushing Hands, Eat Drink Man Woman,* and *Sense and Sensibility* have won critical acclaim. Interest in

Noodles and rice soup or congee (*zhou*) are Taiwanese favorites
for brunch or lunch. Courtesy of Polly Lo.

traditional Chinese music, the different types of classical opera, and folk-
singing have led the Taiwanese to form groups that travel to perform before
fascinated audiences. Taiwanese Americans also display their talent during
Chinese American and Asian American festivals and celebrations and participate in community-wide events, showing that they are a dynamic part of
the American cultural mosaic.

No discussion of the Taiwanese American contribution to America, however, would be complete without a discussion of food. Taiwanese immigrants,
along with those from Hong Kong and China, have introduced the public
to different types of Chinese food. Chinese food has many regional cuisines,
and most Americans were previously most familiar with the Cantonese variety. But other regional cuisines from other parts of China have now been
introduced into the United States to the delight of those who appreciate
Chinese food and the idea that variety is the spice of life. Chinese restaurants
now feature those that specialize in dishes from Sichuan, Beijing, Hunan,
and Shandong. There are also restaurants that offer the Chaozhou and Hakka
types of cuisine. In bringing these regional cuisines to this country, the Taiwanese have served as brokers or midwives in helping to educate the American palate.

Among the different regional cuisines, the Taiwanese variety also deserves
mention. While it can be classified with southern Fujianese cuisine, it also

A wide variety of fresh fish and seafood is available for family meals. Courtesy of Polly Lo.

has some interesting twists because of the fifty years of Japanese occupation from 1895 to 1945. Because Taiwan is an island, it is blessed with an abundance of fish and products from the sea. Shrimp, abalone, scallops, fish, crabs, and squid can be found in many Taiwanese dishes. Chives are used liberally in many of the recipes.

Whereas in the 1950s and early 1960s there were few Taiwanese restaurants, today there are many of them catering to the larger Taiwanese population and the general public. In newspaper ads and on restaurant windows and signs, they proudly proclaim that they serve Taiwanese food and snacks. In the larger restaurants, a premium is placed on fresh seafood. Customers can actually see swimming in tanks the fresh fish that they can select for lunch or dinner. In other tanks there are live prawns, crabs, and lobsters that can also be purchased and prepared as desired. In Asian supermarkets, Taiwanese pickles, condiments, snacks, and baked goods are prominently displayed on the shelves. Gone are the early days when Taiwanese Americans could only snack on instant noodles.

Finally, many Taiwanese Americans from all backgrounds have contributed to the quality of American public life. As good citizens and civic-minded individuals, they serve in community functions. They vote in elections, sit on juries, join in neighborhood group meetings, and join with parent-teacher conferences. They volunteer for projects that help to improve communities and show a concern for their neighbors. Although many perform these roles without calling attention to themselves, many of them do this freely, for they see themselves as residents in America.

The boundaries between a Taiwanese American identity and a Chinese American, Asian American, or American identity are fluid. Among those from Taiwan, some regard themselves only as Taiwanese Americans. Others consider themselves Chinese Americans. Others may be either, depending on the situation. In Taiwan, the perception of difference from China may be contributing to the emergence of a new permanent identity. It may be that ethnogenesis is taking place. But only time can determine whether that is the case. In the meantime, Taiwanese Americans have an identity that is complex and evolving.

NOTE

1. For a somewhat different view, at least for the early phase, see John Robert Shepherd (1993).

Appendix A: Notable Taiwanese Americans

Below are biographical profiles of a few of the many successful Taiwanese Americans.

ELAINE CHAO (1952–)
Former President, United Way of America

Elaine Chao's life is a story of a person possessed with incredible energy and talent. Born in Taibei, she lived in Taiwan until she was eight. Then her mother, her sisters, and she immigrated to the United States in 1961. They came through Los Angeles and then headed for New York where her father was studying for a college degree. When his education was completed, he started a shipping and trading business. He became successful, and as the business expanded, the family was able to move from Queens to a suburban neighborhood in Westchester County.

When Elaine Chao was ready for college, she elected to go to Columbia University but eventually transferred to Mount Holyoke College. Majoring in economics, she did exceptionally well. She graduated in 1975 and went on to Harvard Business School to study business administration. After securing her M.B.A. degree in 1979, she decided to work for Citicorp in New York as an international banker. After several years, she obtained a prestigious White House fellowship to work in the White House in 1983. Afterwards, she took a position with the BankAmerica Capital Markets Group, serving as the vice-president of syndications.

She had captured the eye of government officials, and in 1986 she was offered a position as a deputy administrator with the Federal Maritime Administration. Two years later, she was named chair of the Federal Maritime Commission. In 1989, she was appointed deputy secretary for the U.S. Department of Transportation. In her career with the federal government, she demonstrated that she was an able administrator. Her proven record attracted notice within the Bush Administration, and she was offered the directorship of the Peace Corps in 1991.

As the Peace Corps director, Chao was in a job with high visibility. But her tenure was brief, for George Bush was unable to win reelection. At this point, she accepted another challenge. The United Way of America had been immersed in a large scandal, with accusations of financial improprieties and excessive spending lodged against the organization. Local agencies of the United Way began to abandon the national organization, hoping to distance themselves from the bad publicity. Without dues from the local chapters, the national organization began to founder and was in dire straits.

Hoping to change the direction of the organization, its board undertook the search for a new head. Out of more than six hundred applicants, they selected Chao in 1992 to be their new president and chief executive officer. This post was a challenge filled with many risks and pitfalls. Nonetheless, she was able to get the United Way of America back on track and restore the public's confidence in the organization. She developed a code of ethics, imposed stricter budgetary controls and procedures, and reduced the staff. Within a year, many of the local chapters returned to the fold and paid their national dues. Public contributions to the United Way also were restored to higher levels. With the organization back on a solid footing, she announced her intention to resign in 1996. Shortly after, she accepted a position with the Heritage Foundation, a think-tank in Washington, D.C.

Because of her remarkable record of achievement, many honors have come her way. In 1993, the Harvard Business School presented her with its Alumni Achievement Award. She has received numerous honorary degrees from universities and awards from groups. For all her many accomplishments, she gives full credit to her parents. She has said that they taught her the worth of education and hard work. Active in the Republican party, she is married to Senator Mitch McConnell of Kentucky (Eljera 1996:9; Liu 1996:F9; Gupta 1995b:39–40).

PAUL CHU (1941–   )
Physicist

Superconductivity is a subject that few Americans know much about. Yet it has tremendous potential for technology and science and is the area that has brought Paul Chu worldwide fame. Paul Chu was born in Hunan, China, in 1941, but grew up in Taiwan. In 1962, he graduated from National Chenggong University and came to the United States to study at Fordham University in New York. After receiving his M.S. in 1965, he moved west to earn his Ph.D. from the University of California at San Diego in 1968. His important mentor at this time was Bernd Matthias, a German-born researcher who specialized in superconductivity.

After completing his studies, he taught at Cleveland State University from 1970 to 1979 and rose from assistant to full professor of physics. In 1979, he moved to the University of Houston. His research interests remained in the field of superconductivity. Along with other scientists, he was trying to discover materials which at certain temperatures would lose all resistance. It was well known that at very low temperatures, atomic motion ceases and materials lose all resistance. When that happened, the material could conduct electric current without any loss of energy and thus become a superconductor. The discovery of superconductors would make it possible to deliver power at an extremely low cost, which would be a tremendous scientific breakthrough. It would have many possible commercial applications such as the use of magnets and super high-speed trains.

While most researchers investigated metals for their superconductivity, Chu took a different direction. He worked instead with oxides, which were different but not particularly promising. Oxides are composed of oxygen and metallic elements, but they usually do not conduct electricity. Then, in 1986, he read about some interesting findings by scientists at the research center of IBM in Zurich, Switzerland. Alex Muller and Georg Bednorz had learned that mixing some oxides with other elements and cooling the mixture led to a substantial drop in resistance to electricity.

The findings inspired Chu, and he began experimenting with impure materials having different crystalline structural arrangements. If they could be subjected to extreme pressure, it might raise the temperature to facilitate superconductivity. He collaborated with former student Maw-Kuen Wu at the University of Alabama to test different materials. When the element yttrium was mixed in, there was a dramatic drop in resistance to electricity. In March 1987, when his paper to *Physical Review Letters* was published, it caused a stir. Numerous teams attempted to duplicate the results for superconductivity. They achieved similar results, and the hopes of researchers were raised that a superconductor at room temperature might be found in the future.

The publicity surrounding the discovery brought instant attention to Chu. He was invited to give lectures and presentations at universities and institutes all over the world. Excited by the prospects of Chu's research, the Texas Center for Superconductivity at the University of Houston (TCSUH) was created by the state of Texas to further investigation into this field. A large multidisciplinary team of researchers now work with Chu to study high temperature superconductivity. In addition, many scholars and students seek to study with him, as he is regarded as one of the top researchers in this field.

Many honors have come his way. In 1988, Chu received the prestigious National Medal of Science from President Ronald Reagan and the Comstock Award from the National Academy of Sciences. He became a member of the American Academy of Arts and Sciences and the National Academy of Sciences in 1989. He has been given numerous honorary degrees and has continued to receive awards and commendations. Still actively engaged in research, he is seen by many observers as being a potential Nobel Prize winner (Gleick 1997:29, 30, 55, 74, 77; Sullivan 1987:1, 3; Cowley and Abbott 1988:63).

DAVID HO (1952–   )
Medical Researcher

AIDS or acquired immune deficiency syndrome, is one of the great health problems of the twentieth century. The media, governments, and the public are all concerned about this disease that has killed so many. So far, there is no treatment that will cure or eliminate it, but the work by David Ho is most suggestive and promising.

David Ho was born in 1952 in the city of Taizhong in Taiwan. His parents brought him to the United States when he was twelve. Living in Los Angeles, he initially had difficulty in speaking English. But he eventually succeeded, graduated from high school, and entered the California Institute of Technology. Majoring in physics, he proved to be an excellent student and graduated *summa cum laude* in 1974. Interested in molecular biology, he applied to Harvard Medical School and was accepted. After receiving his medical degree, he decided on a career in academic medicine that focused on research and science.

While doing a residency at Cedars Sinai Hospital in Los Angeles, Ho became interested in the AIDS epidemic. In 1982, to pursue further research on the subject, he chose to study at Massachusetts General Hospital in Boston. Its virology laboratory was led by Martin Hirsch, a renowned scientist who was well known for training young researchers. While working with Hirsch, Ho was able to isolate the HIV virus in the nervous system and semen. He also demonstrated that saliva could not transmit AIDS.

In 1987, Ho moved back to the West Coast and accepted a position at the UCLA Medical School to continue his research. Collaborating with Robert Schooley, he showed that the HIV viral infection was very high in the late stage of AIDS. He agreed to be the director of the Aaron Diamond AIDS Research Center in New York in 1990, so that he could have more resources for his research. During the next year, he published a paper with George Shaw showing that the HIV viral infection was also very high in the initial stage of AIDS but seemed to drop down in the middle stage and become dormant. What had happened to the virus in the middle stage? In 1995, Ho, Schooley, and Shaw demonstrated that in the middle stage, the immune system was desperately struggling to counter the HIV virus.

The 1995 findings were significant. Prior to this time, researchers had thought the AIDS patients were recovering in the middle stage and had conserved on the treatment. New data indicated that the immune system needed medical intervention even in the middle stage when the virus seemed to be in hibernation. But how could the disease be treated? AZT, an anti-retroviral compound of zidovudine that had been touted as a treatment, proved to be inadequate. In a burst of inspiration, Ho thought of using a potent "cocktail" of three antiviral drugs, combining new protease-inhibitor drugs with other medications in the early weeks of infection. The premise is that the HIV virus would have difficulty in mutating to cope with the three drugs. So far, the results seem to be promising, and the HIV in his patients is so low that it cannot be measured.

David Ho's important research landed him on the cover of *Time* magazine as its "Man of the Year." Many other honors have come his way, and he has been asked to join numerous task forces on public health. Despite all this attention, Ho has remained modest and humble. He says that the research on AIDS has always been a collaborative group effort, with all researchers learning from each other (Gorman 1996:56–64; Chua-Eoan 1996/1997:69–70; Hong 1995:113–114).

ANG LEE (1954–   )
Film Director-Producer

Taiwanese Americans and Asian Americans are seen as being strong in science and technology. But what have they done in terms of the arts? Ang Lee is representative of a rising tide of Asian Americans who have made major contributions to the world of film. Like Arthur Dong, Steve Okazaki, Jessica Yu, and Wayne Wang, Ang Lee is turning heads with the artistry he shows in his craft.

Born in Taiwan in 1954, Lee is the son of a school principal, but he took a somewhat different path as he enrolled in the Taiwan Academy of Art where he became interested in acting. In 1978, he decided to come to the United States to study at the University of Illinois at Urbana-Champaign. Because of his lack of fluency in English, he focused on film rather than acting. After graduating with a bachelor of fine arts degree in theater, he moved to the East Coast and studied at New York University for a master's degree in film production.

In New York, he enjoyed immersing himself in learning about films and film production. He completed his studies in 1984, and his thesis film impressed his teachers. When it was entered in the 1985 Film Festival for New York University, *Fine Line* was selected as the best film. But for the next few years, he had little success in attracting notice from movie studio executives. Despite having an agent represent him, it seemed that he was getting nowhere. With no options apparently available to him in the United States, he tried to get support from Taiwan by submitting scripts into a screenplay competition. In 1990, he won the competition sponsored by the government and received a modest sum of money from a Taiwanese production company known as Central Motion Pictures to make a film. In the United States, a production company called Good Machine also became interested in him.

Two years later, Lee came forth with *Pushing Hands*. The words in the Chinese title, *tui shou* or "pushing hands," alluded to *taijiquan* , more popularly known as *taiji* (tai chi) in this country. The plot of the film delved into the experiences of a *taiji* instructor who lives with his son in the United States. Because the father speaks no English, and the son's wife is Caucasian, there are problems stemming from a lack of communication between the two. The film won a Golden Horse Award in Taiwan and enjoyed box office success there as well. It also received Best Film Honors from the Asian Pacific Film Festival in 1991. In 1994, the film was released for showing in the United States.

Continuing to receive support from the two production companies, Lee was able to script and produce the film *The Wedding Banquet* in 1993. It was a bold attempt to deal with the controversial topic of homosexuality, and yet it was endowed with a light comic touch. The film was actually inspired by the experiences of a gay Taiwanese American that Lee knew. It was also partly drawn from the misadventures that took place when Lee married his wife Jane Lin, who had also attended the University of Illinois. The plot centers around a wedding that is held to deceive the parents of the gay Taiwanese and permits humor because of the ruses that are required to fool them. Made for a relatively small sum of money, the film enjoyed great box office success in the United States. It also received critical acclaim, winning the Golden Bear Award for Lee at the Berlin Film Festival. It was also nominated for an Academy Award and a Golden Globe.

Praise continued to come to Lee. In 1994, he released yet another film that he had produced. *Eat Drink Man Woman* was a film that tantalized gourmets and critics alike. The father of three daughters is a chef and he enjoys preparing meals for them. But changes are coming to this family with many surprising twists. In the course of weaving the story, Lee showcases in exquisite detail the dishes that the father prepares. For the shooting of these scenes, several chefs were hired to make the many exotic and authentic dishes. As in the case of his two previous films, *Eat Drink Man Woman* won high praise from critics and moviegoers. It was nominated for the Academy and Golden Globe Awards in the Best Foreign Language Film category. It also was selected as the Best Foreign Language Film by the National Board of Review.

With such favorable exposure, doors began to open everywhere for Ang Lee. One surprise was that he was asked to direct *Sense and Sensibility*, a screenplay by Emma Thompson based on Jane Austen's novel with the same title. Since *Sense and Sensibility* was set in an English context, it was highly unusual to have Lee direct the film. But when the movie was completed in 1995, it drew accolades from audiences and critics. The film was profoundly moving and touching, deeply affecting those who saw it. It was nominated for seven Academy Awards. To many, it signaled that Ang Lee was a director of the first order, of world caliber. While he has directed only five films, every one has been a gem. Each has won praise and admiration from critics and viewers alike ("Lee, Ang" 1997:31–34; Henry 1995:180–81).

YUAN-TSE LEE (1936–   )
Chemist

It is said that science knows no boundaries. Yuan-tse Lee has made contributions to both the United States and his native Taiwan. A Nobel Prize winner in chemistry, he has continued to champion the advancement of science and research in both countries.

Yuan-tse Lee (Li Yuanze) was born in Xinzhu, Taiwan, in 1936. His father was a well-known painter, but Lee did not follow in his footsteps. As a schoolboy, he had chanced upon a book about the famed Polish-born French researcher, Marie Sklodowska Curie. A distinguished scientist, she had won two Nobel prizes, one for physics and one for chemistry. It was a remarkable feat. Impressed by what he had read, Lee decided to pursue a career in science just like Curie.

An excellent high school student, Lee went on to study at National Taiwan University. Upon graduation in 1959, he continued his interest in chemistry by securing a master's degree at National Qinghua University in Taiwan in 1961. Many students from Taiwan were desirous of pursuing advanced study and research in the United States, and Lee fit into the same pattern. He enrolled at the University of California at Berkeley in 1962 to begin his doctoral studies. His specialty was the chemical ionization of electrically excited alkali atoms. After receiving his Ph.D. in 1965, he went to the East Coast to work with Professor Dudley Herschbach of Harvard University.

Herschbach was also interested in the reaction dynamics of alkali atoms. Experimenting with beams of molecules colliding at high speeds, he was investigating the processes by which new molecular combinations occur. Working with Herschbach, Lee designed a mass-spectrometer that could identify the paths of different ions after they separated. It was a crossed molecular beams method using magnetic and electric fields to help in the deflection and identification of the ions in chemical reactions. For this work, Lee and Herschbach would receive the Nobel Prize in Chemistry in 1986. They shared the prize with John Polanyi of the University of Toronto who had investigated the same problem but had used another method.

In his academic career, Lee taught at the University of Chicago from 1968 to 1974 and rose from assistant professor to full professor during that time. Then, in 1974, he returned to the University of California at Berkeley where he had done his doctoral work. He was both a professor of chemistry at the university and the principal investigator at the Lawrence Livermore Laboratory, guiding many students and colleagues in their research.

In 1993, Lee accepted an offer from President Li Denghui to head Taiwan's Academia Sinica. The organization was the Republic of China's most prestigious academic organization. Returning to Taibei, Lee has faced the challenge of trying to elevate the scientific and research position of Taiwan. He has been active in efforts to raise funds to expand research on many different fronts. He has also devoted a lot of energy to recruiting eminent

overseas Chinese and Taiwanese scientists, technicians, and other professionals to return to Taiwan. He hopes that with their presence, Taiwan can be
transformed into an international center for cutting edge science and technology (Wu 1995:205–6).

CHANG-LIN TIEN (1935–)
Former University Administrator

For a foreign-born immigrant, it was like a Horatio Alger story. He had come
to study in America, and he seemed to be on track for a career as a respected
university professor. But after several years, Chang-lin Tien was made president of the University of California at Berkeley, one of the preeminent
research institutions in the world. It was almost too much to believe.

Chang-lin Tien was born in Wuhan, China, in 1935. Because of war with
Japan after 1937, his family moved to Shanghai. To escape the civil war in
China between the Nationalist and Communist forces, his family fled to
Taiwan in 1949. An excellent student, Tien had no difficulty in graduating
from National Taiwan University in 1955 with a degree in mechanical engineering. Desiring further study, he came to the United States and entered
the University of Louisville to work toward an M.A. degree. Upon completing the requirements for his degree in 1957, he enrolled at Princeton
University where he would receive his M.A. and Ph.D. in mechanical engineering in 1959.

Tien accepted an offer to teach at the University of California at Berkeley
and conducted specialized research in thermal radiation. He made a name
for himself in this area and received many awards and honors for his work.
He was a Guggenheim Fellow in 1965–66 and an Alexander von Humboldt
Foundation fellow in Germany in 1979. But in 1983, his career took a
different turn. He became the vice-chancellor for research at the university.
His experience opened the door for him to become the vice-chancellor at the
University of California at Irvine in 1988. At Irvine, he was known as an
able administrator who worked well with faculty and students.

His successes as a university administrator attracted notice. In 1990, he
was asked to return to the University of California at Berkeley to be its
chancellor. This made him the head of one of the most prestigious universities in the world. He therefore joined a very small circle of Asian Americans
who had served as university heads. These included Fujio Matsuda of the
University of Hawaii, and S. I. Hayakawa and Chia-wei Woo of San Fran-

cisco State University. But clearly, Tien commanded unparalleled attention as the head of an elite research university.

Tien was fully aware of the importance of his post. However, he under-stood how the heart of a university worked, and he recruited brilliant young faculty. He also worked tirelessly and successfully to raise funds for the uni-versity. He was particularly effective in securing funds from corporations, alumni, and countries in Asia and the Pacific Rim. Despite his busy schedule, he earned a reputation as a compassionate and caring administrator who took walks across campus to chat with students, their parents, and faculty. He also attended meetings and forums to increase his ties with the community and the public.

As an administrator, Tien has demonstrated leadership and vision on mat-ters of broad national and international concern. He believes that the future of the United States lies in diversity and multiculturalism. Consequently, he has argued on behalf of affirmative understanding and has been an advocate for the improvement of race and ethnic relations in the United States. In the international arena, he believes that Asia and the Pacific Rim will be impor-tant in the global economy and the peace of the world. For this reason, he encourages dialogue and engagement with the Asian countries across the Pacific.

In 1996, Tien announced that he planned to step down from the post of chancellor in 1997. He said that he planned to return to being a faculty member at the university. In the comments that followed his announcement, many observers commended him for his superlative efforts to help the Uni-versity of California at Berkeley maintain its prominence during a severe recession in the state. Others praised him for being a farsighted educator and national leader, who also served as an admirable role model for Asian Amer-icans (Yip 1996:13–15; Wong 1997:15; Gupta 1995a:375–77).

Appendix B: Tables

Table 1
Selected Ethnic and Foreign-Born Populations from Asia in 1990

Ethnic Group	Total U.S. Population
Chinese*	1,645,472
Filipino	1,406,770
Japanese	847,562
Indian	815,447
Korean	798,849
Vietnamese	614,547
Laotian	149,014
Cambodian	147,411
Hmong	90,082
Thai	91,275

Source: U.S. Bureau of the Census. 1992. *1990 Census of the Population, General Population Characteristics, United States,* Table 253.

*Chinese foreign-born population includes those from China, Hong Kong, and Taiwan.

Table 2
Immigrants from Taiwan, Hong Kong, China, and Singapore
Admitted by Region and Country of Birth to U.S.: Fiscal Years
1984–1994

	Taiwan	Hong Kong	China	Singapore
1984	12,478	5,465	23,363	377
1985	14,895	5,171	24,787	460
1986	13,424	5,021	25,106	480
1987	11,931	4,706	25,841	469
1988	9,670	8,546	28,717	492
1989	13,974	9,740	32,272	566
1990	15,151	9,393	31,815	620
1991	13,274	10,427	33,025	535
1992	16,344	10,452	38,907	774
1993	14,329	9,161	65,578	798
1994	10,032	7,731	53,985	542

Source: U.S. Immigration and Naturalization Service. 1996. *Statistical Yearbook of the Immigration and Naturalization Service, 1994*, Table 3.

Table 3
Immigrants Admitted by Selected Class of Admission and Region and Selected Country of Last Permanent Residence: Fiscal Year 1994

Region and Country of Last Permanent Residence	Total	Family-Sponsored Preferences	Employment-Based Preferences	Immediate Relatives of U.S. Citizens
Taiwan	11,168	4,131	3,780	3,165
Hong Kong	11,953	6,367	2,583	2,392
China	47,699	7,308	31,913	7,711
Singapore	758	74	286	339
India	33,173	15,650	7,715	9,100
Japan	6,974	243	2,411	3,455
Korea	15,417	4,640	4,241	6,390
Philippines	52,832	14,844	9,171	27,220
Thailand	15,131	1,356	367	2,138
Vietnam	32,387	2,799	33	3,668

Source: U.S. Immigration and Naturalization Service. 1996. *Statistical Yearbook of the Immigration and Naturalization Service, 1994*, Table 9.

Note: There are several other classes of admission, so the sums of the family-sponsored preferences, employment-based preferences, and the immediate relatives category do not equal the totals listed in the left-hand column.

Table 4
Immigrants Admitted by Selected Class of Admission and Region and Selected Country of Last Permanent Residence: Fiscal Year 1994

Region and Country of Last Permanent Residence	Taiwan	Hong Kong	China
Total	11,168	11,953	47,699
Family-Sponsored Preferences	4,131	6,367	7,308
Employment-Based Preferences	3,780	2,583	31,913
Immediate Relatives of U.S. Citizens			
Total	3,165	2,392	7,711
Spouses	1,301	1,098	2,923
Children	308	180	1,132
Parents	1,556	1,114	3,656

Source: U.S. Immigration and Naturalization Service. 1996. *Statistical Yearbook of the Immigration and Naturalization Service, 1994,* Table 9.

Note: There are several other classes of admission, so the sums of the family-sponsored preferences, employment-based preferences, and immediate relatives of U.S. citizens do not equal the totals listed in the first row of figures.

Table 5
Immigrants Admitted Who Were Adjusted to Permanent Resident Status by Selected Status at Entry and Region and Selected Country of Birth: Fiscal Year 1994

	Taiwan	Hong Kong	China
Total	4,578	1,913	35,453
Visitors for business	107	44	670
Visitors for pleasure	1,270	573	4,277
Students	1,264	496	15,206
Temporary workers	1,156	416	5,535
Exchange visitors	48	22	4,257
Fiances, fiancees	31	41	393
Intracompany transfers	331	148	628
Refugees and parolees	20	90	2,370
Entered without inspection	6	2	140
Other and unknown	345	81	1,977

Source: U.S. Immigration and Naturalization Service. 1996. *Statistical Yearbook of the Immigration and Naturalization Service, 1994*, Table 10.

Table 6

Immigrant New Arrivals Admitted by Selected Port of Entry and Region and Selected Country of Birth: Fiscal Year 1994

Region and Country of Birth	Chicago	Los Angeles	Newark	New York	San Francisco
Taiwan	117	2,377	361	597	1,299
Hong Kong	187	1,505	63	1,016	2,114
China	757	4,068	137	5,004	5,982
Singapore	8	89	3	25	54
India	2,953	2,723	528	10,920	2,500
Japan	115	903	53	317	392
Korea	935	3,368	10	2,195	907
Philippines	1,929	13,943	146	3,034	10,104
Thailand	81	669	9	161	247

Source: U.S. Immigration and Naturalization Service. 1996. *Statistical Yearbook of the Immigration and Naturalization Service, 1994*, Table 16.

Table 7
Immigrants Admitted by Selected Country of Birth and Selected States of Intended Residence: Fiscal Year 1994

State of Intended Residence	Taiwan	Hong Kong	China
Total for All States	10,032	7,731	53,985
California	4,862	3,359	17,447
Florida	179	167	871
Georgia	115	65	522
Hawaii	81	239	743
Illinois	247	216	1,684
Maryland	2,144	118	1,620
Massachusetts	140	243	1,995
Michigan	141	55	663
New Jersey	580	285	2,174
New York	851	1,318	11,745
North Carolina	89	57	468
Ohio	144	63	872
Pennsylvania	182	105	1,621
Texas	743	298	1,932
Virginia	163	115	971
Washington	206	285	842

Source: U.S. Immigration and Naturalization Service. 1996. *Statistical Yearbook of the Immigration and Naturalization Service, 1994*, Table 17.

Note: Total includes all 50 states, the District of Columbia, and U.S. territories and possessions.

Table 8
Immigrants Admitted by Selected Country of Birth and Selected
Metropolitan Statistical Area of Intended Residence: Fiscal Year 1994

	Taiwan	Hong Kong	China
Total	7,378	5,707	36,721
Los Angeles-Long Beach	2,342	1,067	6,183
San Jose	788	272	1,945
New York	653	1,159	10,163
Orange County	555	136	827
Oakland	347	525	2,327
Washington, DC-MD-VA	333	161	1,849
Houston	330	176	846
San Francisco	317	909	3,934
Chicago	224	201	1,420
Middlesex-Somerset-Hunterdon, NJ	187	73	621
Seattle-Bellevue-Everett, WA	183	245	667
Dallas	169	65	433
San Diego	142	73	631
Riverside-San Bernardino, CA	142	57	256
Newark	133	70	465
Boston-Lawrence-Lowell-Brockton	118	221	1,727
Nassau-Suffolk, NY	110	82	589
Bergen-Passaic, NJ	109	56	352
Philadelphia, PA-NJ	104	102	1,107
Atlanta	92	57	379

Source: U.S. Immigration and Naturalization Service. 1996. *Statistical Yearbook of the Immigration and Naturalization Service, 1994*, Table 19.

Table 9
Immigrants Admitted by Major Occupation Group and Region and Selected Country of Birth: Fiscal Year 1994

	Taiwan	Hong Kong	China
Total	10,032	7,731	53,985
Occupation			
Total	3,948	3,058	21,462
Professional specialty and technical	1,636	872	7,272
Executive, administrative, and managerial	1,273	969	2,993
Sales	165	125	729
Administrative support	506	580	1,721
Precision production, craft, and repair	37	174	676
Operator, fabricator, and laborer	57	92	2,159
Farming, forestry, and fishing	43	2	2,248
Service	231	244	3,664
No occupation or not reported	6,084	4,673	32,523

Source: U.S. Immigration and Naturalization Service. 1996. *Statistical Yearbook of the Immigration and Naturalization Service, 1994*, Table 21.

Table 10
Persons Naturalized by Region and Selected Country of Former
Allegiance: Fiscal Years 1985–1994

	Taiwan	China
1985	3,407	11,743
1986	4,501	11,151
1987	4,033	9,208
1988	5,716	10,509
1989	5,779	11,664
1990	6,895	13,563
1991	10,876	16,783
1992	6,408	13,488
1993	7,384	16,851
1994	9,450	20,828

Source: U.S. Immigration and Naturalization Service. 1996. *Statistical Yearbook of the Immigration and Naturalization Service, 1994*, Table 48.

Table 11
Immigrants Admitted from Top Twenty Countries of Birth: Fiscal Year 1994

Category of Admission	1994	1993	Change Number	Percent
All countries	804,416	904,292	−99,876	−11.0
1. Mexico	111,398	126,561	−15,163	−12.0
2. China	53,985	65,578	−11,593	−17.7
3. Philippines	53,535	63,457	−9,922	−15.6
4. Dominican Republic	51,189	45,420	5,769	12.7
5. Vietnam	41,345	59,614	−18,269	−30.6
6. India	34,921	40,121	−5,200	−13.0
7. Poland	28,048	27,846	202	.7
8. Ukraine	21,010	18,316	2,694	14.7
9. El Salvador	17,644	26,818	−9,174	−34.2
10. Ireland	17,256	13,590	3,666	27.0
11. United Kingdom	16,326	18,783	−2,457	−13.1
12. Canada	16,068	17,156	−1,088	−6.3
13. Korea	16,011	18,026	−2,015	−11.2
14. Russia	15,249	12,079	3,170	26.2
15. Cuba	14,727	13,666	1,061	7.8
16. Jamaica	14,349	17,241	−2,892	−16.8
17. Haiti	13,333	10,094	3,239	32.1
18. Iran	11,422	14,841	−3,419	−23.0
19. Colombia	10,847	12,819	−1,972	−15.4
20. Taiwan	10,032	14,329	−4,297	−30.0
Other	235,721	267,937	−32,216	−12.0

Source: U.S. Immigration and Naturalization Service. 1996. *Statistical Yearbook of the Immigration and Naturalization Service, 1994*, Table D.

Bibliography

Bachrack, Stanley D. 1976. *The Committee of One Million*. New York: Columbia University Press.

Berman, Daniel K. 1992. *Words Like Colored Glass: The Role of the Press in Taiwan's Democratization Process*. Boulder, Colo.: Westview Press.

Bryant, Daniel. 1992. "The Why and Why Not of Pinyin—A Response to De-Francis." *Journal of the Chinese Language Teachers Association* 27:111–14.

Busto, Rudy V. 1996. "The Gospel According to the Model Minority?: Hazarding an Interpretation of Asian American Evangelical Students." *Amerasia Journal* 22:133–47.

Chai, Trong R. 1981. "The Murder of an American University Professor in Taiwan." *Letter on Taiwan*, no. 5:8–9.

Chen, Elsa. 1997. "SGN Introduction Letter." http://www.csupomona.edu/arch/FAPA/sgn.html, May 15.

Chen, Hsiang-shui. 1992. *Chinatown No More: Taiwan Immigrants in Contemporary New York*. Ithaca: Cornell University Press.

Chen, Yu-hsi. 1995. "The Dual Role of the Chinese Press in the United States: Change and Continuity." *Bulletin of the Committee of Concerned Asian Scholars* 27:37–47.

Chinese American Librarians Association, Midwest Chapter. 1995. *Midwest Area Chinese American Resources Guide*. Greencastle, Ind.: Midwest Chapter, Chinese American Librarians Association.

Chua-Eoan, Howard. 1996/1997. "The Tao of Ho." *Time*, December 30, 1996/January 6, 1997, pp. 69–70.

"Chuang Yen." 1997. http://shellz.ba.best.com/~shawny/buddhism/baus/, May 10.

Cohen, Marc J. 1988. *Taiwan at the Crossroads: Human Rights, Political Development, and Social Change on the Beautiful Island*. Washington, D.C.: Asia Resource Center.

Cowley, Geoffrey, and Nonny Abbott. 1988. "The Superman of Superconductivity." *Newsweek*, December 19, p. 63.

Dai, Mingkang, and Lingan Bai. 1997. "National Cheng Kung University Alumni Meeting." *World Journal*, May 18, p. B3.

DeFrancis, John. 1990. "The Why of Pinyin Grapheme Selection." *Journal of the Chinese Language Teachers Association* 25:1–14.

Eljera, Bert. 1996. "Newsmaker: Elaine Chao." *Asianweek*, May 31, p. 9.

Fong, Timothy. 1994. *The First Suburban Chinatown: The Remaking of Monterey Park, California*. Philadelphia: Temple University Press.

Gleick, James. 1997. "In the Trenches of Science." *New York Times Magazine*, August 16, pp. 29, 30, 55, 74, 77.

Gorman, Christine. 1997. "The Disease Detective." *Time*, December 30, 1996/ January 6, pp. 56–64.

Gupta, Himanee. 1995a. "Chang-lin Tien." In *Notable Asian Americans*, ed. Helen Zia and Susan B. Gall, pp. 375–77. Detroit: Gale Research.

———. 1995b. "Elaine Chao." In *Notable Asian Americans*, ed. Helen Zia and Susan B. Gall, pp. 39–40. Detroit: Gale Research.

Harrell, Stevan, and Chun-chieh Huang, ed. 1994. *Cultural Change in Postwar Taiwan*. Boulder, Colo.: Westview Press.

"Harvard Taiwanese Students Association." 1997. http://hcs.harvard.edu/~taiwan/ acts.html, April 29.

"Hawaiian History." 1995. *Formosan Quarterly*, no. 22, August:1–2.

Henry, Jim. "Ang Lee." 1995. In *Notable Asian Americans*, ed. Helen Zia and Susan B. Gall, pp. 180–81. Detroit: Gale Research.

Hoexter, Corinne K. 1976. *From Canton to California: The Epic of Chinese Immigration*. New York: Four Winds Press.

Hong, Terry. 1995. "David D. Ho." In *Notable Asian Americans*, ed. Helen Zia and Susan B. Gall, pp. 113–14. Detroit: Gale Research.

Horton, John. 1995. *The Politics of Diversity: Immigration, Resistance, and Change in Monterey Park, California*. Philadelphia: Temple University Press.

Hsieh, Chiao-min. 1964. *Taiwan-Ilha Formosa: A Geography in Perspective*. Washington, D.C.: Butterworths.

Huang, Caroline. 1994. "Chinese-Language and Foreign-Language Instruction in California Schools." In *Origins and Destinations: 41 Essays on Chinese America*, pp. 385–87. Los Angeles: Chinese Historical Society of Southern California and UCLA Asian American Studies Center.

Huang, Zhonglin. 1996. "The Secret Worry about *Guoyu zhuyin fuhao*." *World Journal*, January 14, p. S3.

Hwang, David Henry. 1990. *FOB and Other Plays*. New York: Plume.

Kaplan, David E. 1992. *Fires of the Dragon: Politics, Murder, and the Kuomintang*. New York: Atheneum.

Koen, Ross Y. 1974. *The China Lobby in American Politics*. New York: Harper and Row.

"Kumon Math Promotes English Curriculum to Accompany Children's Growth."
    1995. *World Journal*, October 5, p. B19.

Lai, Him Mark. 1987. "The Chinese-American Press." In *The Ethnic Press in the
    United States: A Historical Analysis and Handbook*, ed. Sally M. Miller, pp.
    27–43. New York: Greenwood Press.

———. 1990. "The Chinese Press in the United States and Canada Since World
    War II: A Diversity of Voices." In *Chinese America: History and Perspectives,
    1990*. pp. 107–55. San Francisco: Chinese Historical Society of America.

———. 1996. "Chinese Organizations in America Based on Locality of Origin and/
    or Dialect-Group Affiliation, 1940s–1990s." In *Chinese America: History and
    Perspectives, 1996*. pp. 19–92. San Francisco: Chinese Historical Society of
    America.

Lai, Him Mark, Genny Lim, and Judy Yung, eds. 1980. *Island: Poetry and History
    of Chinese Immigrants on Angel Island, 1910–1940*. San Francisco: Hoc Doi.

"Lee, Ang." 1997. *Current Biography* 58:31–34.

Lee, Helen. 1996. "Silent Exodus: Can the East Asian Church in America Reverse
    the Flight of its Next Generation?" *Christianity Today* 40:50–53.

Li, Suqiu, and Chunhui Lin. 1996. "Invitation to the 1996 Eighth Meeting of the
    North American Taiwanese Women's Association." *Taiwan Tribune*, March
    27, p. 7.

Lin, Diana. 1996a. "As Buddhism Grows, So Grows Its Impact." *Free China Journal*,
    June 14, p. 7.

———. 1996b. "The Torchbearer: Taiwan-born Conductor in U.S. Holds Baton
    High to Promote Chinese Orchestral Music." *Free China Journal*, June 28,
    p. 5.

Lin, Irene. 1996. "Journey to the Far West: Chinese Buddhism in America." *Amer-
    asia Journal* 22:107–32.

Liu, Caitlin. 1996. "A Double Dose of Work." *New York Times*, September 8,
    p. F9.

Ma, L. Eve Armentrout. 1990. *Revolutionaries, Monarchists, and Chinatowns: Chinese
    Politics in the Americas and the 1911 Revolution*. Honolulu: University of
    Hawaii Press.

"A Mother and Child." 1996. *World Journal*, August 11, p. 5.

"Native Tribes Want 'Dignified' Name." 1992. *Free China Journal*, May 22, p. 2.

Newman, Robert P. 1983. "Clandestine Chinese Nationalist Efforts to Punish Their
    American Detractors." *Diplomatic History* 7:205–22.

North American Taiwanese Women's Association, Northern California, and Tai-
    wanese American Citizens League, Northern California. 1995. *Taiwanese
    Homestyle Cooking: A Guide to Taiwanese Cooking*. Palo Alto, Calif.: North
    American Taiwanese Women's Association, Northern California, and Tai-
    wanese American Citizens League, Northern California Chapter.

North American Taiwanese Engineers Association. 1997. "Program: Science and
    Technology in Academia Sinica and Beyond." *World Journal*, April 12,
    p. B6.

"Northwestern Taiwanese Students Association." 1997. http://www.nwu.edu/tasc. html, May 28.

"The 1997 Overseas Chinese Youth and Teenagers Language Training and Study Tour to the Republic of China." 1997. *World Journal*, February 24, p. B8.

Palinkas, Lawrence A. 1984. "Social Fission and Cultural Change in an Ethnic Chinese Church." *Ethnic Groups* 5:255–77.

Park, Michael. 1981. "Taiwan Haunted by Ghost of Educator." *Los Angeles Times*, October 7, pp. 2–4.

Peterson, Andrew J. 1995. "The Development of a New Chinatown: Post-1965 Changes in New York's Chinatown." In *Chinese America: History and Perspectives, 1995*, pp. 199–214. San Francisco: Chinese Historical Society of America.

"Professor Chen Wen-Chen's Memorial Foundation." 1997. *Taiwan Tribune*, March 8, p. 8.

"Republic of China 1997 Summer Overseas Language Training and Study Tour." 1997. *World Journal*, February 24, p. B8.

Rubinstein, Murray A. 1991. "Taiwanese Protestantism in Time and Space, 1865–1988." In *Taiwan: Economy, Society and History*, ed. E. K. Y. Chen, Jack F. Williams, and Joseph Wang, pp. 250–82. Hong Kong: Centre of Asian Studies, University of Hong Kong Press.

———, ed. 1994. *The Other Taiwan: 1945 to the Present.* Armonk, N.Y.: M.E. Sharpe.

Sheng, Virginia. 1997. "Demographic Changes Reported." *Free China Journal*, April 11, p. 4.

Shepherd, John Robert. 1993. *Statecraft and Political Economy on the Taiwan Frontier, 1600–1800.* Stanford: Stanford University Press.

"Southeast Bay Taiwanese Association Celebrates Mother's Day on the 18th." 1996. *World Journal*, May 8, p. B6.

Su, Christie. 1995. "Education Reform Turns to New Chapter." *Free China Journal*, August 11, p. 7.

Sullivan, Walter. 1987. "Team Reports Breakthrough in Conductivity of Electricity." *New York Times*, February 16, p. 1.

"Taiwan Harassment of Students in U.S. Reported." 1981. *Los Angeles Times*, July 31, p. 23.

"Taiwanese Association's New Year's Eve Festival Program Is Rich and Varied." 1996. *World Journal*, January 13, p. 27.

"Taiwanese Students at Stanford Reportedly Spy on Each Other." 1982. *San Francisco Chronicle*, October 8, p. 8.

Tenorio, Vyvyan. 1981. "In Taiwan, the Kuomintang Shows a Visitor Dissent Can Be Deadly." *Los Angeles Times*, September 13, p. IV-3.

"Tih-Wu Wang, 84, Publisher of Taiwan Paper." 1996. *New York Times*, March 24, p. 19.

Trudeau, Garry. 1996. "Doonesbury." *Honolulu Star-Bulletin*, June 25, p. A9.

Tseng, Yen-Fen. 1994. Suburban Ethnic Economy: Chinese Business Communities in Los Angeles. Ph.D. diss., University of California, Los Angeles.

————. 1995. "Beyond 'Little Taipei': The Development of Taiwanese Immigrant Businesses in Los Angeles." *International Migration Review* 29:33–58.

Tucker, Nancy Bernkopf. 1994. *Taiwan, Hong Kong, and the United States, 1945–1992: Uncertain Friendships.* New York: Twayne Publishers.

Tyson, James. 1967. "Christians and the Taiwanese Independence Movement: A Commentary." *Asian Affairs* 14:163–170.

"Tzu Chi." 1997. http://www.tzuchi.org/, May 10.

U.S. Bureau of the Census. 1992. *1990 Census of the Population, General Population Characteristics, United States.* Washington, D.C.: Government Printing Office.

————. 1993. *Asian and Pacific Islanders in the United States. 1990 Census of Population.* Washington, D.C.: Government Printing Office.

————. 1993. *The Foreign-Born Population in the United States. 1990 Census of Population.* Washington, D.C.: Government Printing Office.

U.S. Immigration and Naturalization Service. 1996. *Statistical Yearbook of the Immigration and Naturalization Service, 1994.* Washington, D.C.: Government Printing Office.

Wachman, Alan M. 1994. *Taiwan: National Identity and Democratization.* Armonk, N.Y.: M.E. Sharpe.

Wang, Wayne. 1994. *Chan is Missing,* ed. Diane Mark. Honolulu: Bamboo Ridge Press.

Wong, Edward. 1997. "Optimal Equilibrium." *Asianweek,* January 31, p. 15.

"World Journal Twentieth Anniversary Special Edition." 1996. *World Journal,* February 12, pp. D1–2.

Wu, Douglas. 1995. "Yuan T. Lee." In *Notable Asian Americans,* ed. Helen Zia and Susan B. Gall, pp. 205–6. Detroit: Gale Research.

Xiao Di [pen name]. 1997. "Is It Necessary to Learn Chinese?" *World Journal,* April 20, p. C10.

"Yale Taiwanese Students Association." 1997. http://www.yale.edu/taiwan/about-club.html, April 29.

Yip, Alethea. 1996. "Chancellor Tien Steps Down." *Asianweek,* July 12, pp. 13–15.

Yun, Eugenia. 1997. "The Great Awakening." *Free China Review* 47:4–11.

Zhou, Min. 1992. *Chinatown: The Socioeconomic Potential of an Urban Enclave.* Philadelphia: Temple University Press.

Index

dren, 32, 41–43, 53; stereotypes about students, 43–44
Educational Testing Service (ETS), 44
Er er ba. See February 28 Incident

Family: marriage, 32–35; role of children, 26– 27; in Taiwan, 27–28; in United States, 28–31; values, 31–33
February 28 Incident (1947), 10, 104–5
Federation of Alumni of Chinese Universities and Institutes, 59
Festivals, 95–96, 119; Clear and Bright Festival, 100; Double Ninth Festival, 100; Double Seventh Festival, 100; Dragon Boat Festival, 98–99; Ghost Month Festival, 101; Lantern Festival, 98; Lunar New Year, 96–98; Mid-Autumn Festival, 99–100; Winter Solstice Festival, 100–101. *See also* Guanyin; Mazu
Fiancees Act (1946), 15
"Five Relationships," 25
Flushing, New York, 21
FOB, 118
Foguangshan, 87–89
Fong, Hiram, 119
Formosan Association for Human Rights (FAHR), 68, 108–9
Formosan Association for Public Affairs (FAPA), 67, 85, 109, 116
Formosan Christians for Self-Determination, 108
Formosan Club of America, 109
Formosan Quarterly, 113
"Four Young Tigers," 11
Fujian province, 2–5, 8

Gaoxiong, 5
Gaoxiong Incident, 107
Giles, Herbert, 47
Greater China, 103
Guangdong province, 2, 4–5, 8
Guan Gong, 7

Guanxi, 55
Guanyin, 7, 101
Guomindang. See Nationalist Party
Guoyu Luomazi, 48
Guoyu Zhuyin Fuhao, 47–49

Hakka: dialect, 5; identity, 2, 4; organizations, 58–59; relations with Fujianese, 2, 115
Hakka Fellow Townsmen's Association of America, 58
Hammer, Susan, 82
Han Chinese, 1
Hanyu Pinyin, 48–49, 52
Harris, Michael D., 82
Hart-Celler Act (1965). *See* Immigration and Nationality Act of 1965
Hawaiian Sovereignty Movement, 114–15
Henan, 4
Ho, David, 122
Hokkien, 5
Hong Kong, 11, 62, 113; immigrants, 20
Houston, 21–22, 57, 69, 87, 89
Hualian, 88
Huang, Helen, 40
Hwang, David Henry, 118–19

Identity: *Han* Chinese, 1; native place, 1–2. *See also* Taiwanese Identity
"Ilha Formosa," 3
Immigration. *See* Chinese Immigration; Taiwanese Immigration
Immigration Act of 1990, 18–19
Immigration and Nationality Act of 1965, 15–17
Institutional completeness, 24
Intercollegiate Taiwanese American Students Association (ITASA), 63
Intergroup relations, 118–21
Intermarriage, 16, 33
International Daily News, 73–74, 79
Internet, 85–86, 113

About the Author

FRANKLIN NG is Professor of Anthropology at California State University, Fresno. He is the former editor of the *Journal of American-East Asian Relations* and is also on the editorial board of the *Amerasia Journal* and the *Journal of American Ethnic History*.